A SKEPTIC'S CASE
FOR NUCLEAR DISARMAMENT

A SKEPTIC'S CASE
FOR NUCLEAR DISARMAMENT

MICHAEL E. O'HANLON

BROOKINGS INSTITUTION PRESS
Washington, D.C.

Library of Congress Cataloging-in-Publication data

O'Hanlon, Michael E.
  A skeptic's case for nuclear disarmament / Michael O'Hanlon.
    p.   cm.
  Includes bibliographical references and index.
  Summary: "An endorsement for nuclear disarmament, especially the dismantling of existing bomb inventories, but with caveats relating to threats posed by nations or groups inside the agreement framework who do not abide by it and those outside who have never allied themselves with those advocating a nuclear-free world"—Provided by publisher.
  ISBN 978-0-8157-0507-9 (hardcover : alk. paper)
  1. Nuclear disarmament. I. Title.
  JZ5675.O43 2010
  327.1'747—dc22   2010026368

9 8 7 6 5 4 3 2 1

Printed on acid-free paper

Typeset in Sabon

Composition by Cynthia Stock
Silver Spring, Maryland

Printed by R. R. Donnelley
Harrisonburg, Virginia

To
HAL FEIVESON
and
FRANK VON HIPPEL

CONTENTS

FOREWORD

FOR THE PAST SIXTEEN years, Mike O'Hanlon has been a rare and valued asset—not just to Brookings but to the nation and the world. He combines expertise based on fact-based research with intellectual passion for his subject, which is nothing less than war and peace—how to prepare for, and sometimes prosecute, the former, and how to preserve the latter.

Much of Mike's prolific and high-impact work has been in the realm of what is called, rather inadequately, "conventional" warfare. He has made about a dozen trips to the Balkans, Afghanistan, and Iraq and published two books just on those conflicts.

But Mike is also an acute student of the technology and theology of nuclear warfare—which, because of the nature of the weapons, is largely the study of preserving the nuclear peace. For decades, that goal was advanced through a combination of arms control agreements and the paradoxical concept of deterrence, or what our late trustee Robert McNamara famously dubbed "mutual assured destruction."

Starting with Harry Truman, several presidents or their advisers have contemplated and, in some cases, advocated the elimination of nuclear weaponry. Jimmy Carter, for example, called for the "elimination of all nuclear weapons from this Earth" in his

1977 inaugural address, and later Carter worked with his Russian counterpart, Leonid Brezhnev, to draft and sign the SALT II Treaty, which aimed to further reduce the nuclear arsenals of both countries. Taking another tact, Ronald Reagan promoted the "Star Wars" defense as a means of rendering offensive missiles "impotent and obsolete." But even as the Soviets were building up their own superpower arsenal, they paid lip service to "general and complete disarmament." That goal is enshrined in the Nuclear Non-Proliferation Treaty (NPT) that went into force forty years ago—and which has the standing of law for the United States.

However, until recently, most policymakers and much of the national security elite regarded the idea of "global zero" as a fantasy—and a potentially dangerous one if it were ever incorporated into policy, diplomacy, or strategy.

That has begun to change, largely because of the initiative of two former secretaries of state, one former secretary of defense, and one former senator representing both major parties. In January 2007 Henry Kissinger, George Shultz, William Perry, and Sam Nunn published an article in the *Wall Street Journal* urging abolition of nuclear weapons and promoted the idea publicly over the years that followed. President Obama endorsed the goal in his campaign, proclaimed it as a guiding principle of his defense policy as president, and persuaded his Russian counterpart, Dmitri Medvedev, to endorse it in their first bilateral meeting on April 1, 2009.

With this book, Mike enters the debate as a self-described skeptic who nonetheless believes that however long it takes, the leaders of the world must consciously, patiently, and prudently move in the direction of zero. Nuclear weapons, he believes, are just too dangerous to treat as usable instruments of war. The longer they remain fixtures on the international security landscape, the greater the danger that they will be used by inadvertence, or in a guns-of-August scenario that spins out of control. Either that, or they will fall into the hands of terrorists or nonstate actors like al Qaeda. Moreover, they will exacerbate the flammable dynamics of rivalries like the one between India and Pakistan—nuclear weapons states that have long refused to sign the NPT on the grounds that it discriminates in favor of the United States, Russia, China, Britain, and France. If those five countries—the NPT-authorized "nuclear-haves"—were pursuing serious reductions in the near term and global zero in the long term, it might be easier to keep the nuclear have-nots (including the nuclear "wannabe" Iran) from developing bombs of their own and eventually to coax India, Pakistan, Israel, and North Korea into a global nonproliferation regime.

But in making this case for abolition, Mike employs his realism as a defense analyst as well as his training as a physicist to stress how hard it will be to get to zero—and how long it will take. Eradication would have to be verifiable. The "renaissance" in peaceful nuclear energy—driven in part by concerns about climate change—requires the strengthening of an NPT that is now in danger of unraveling. The specter of other weapons of mass destruction—biological and chemical—are an additional impediment to retiring the concept and practice of nuclear deterrence.

But just as it is a mistake to let the perfect be the enemy of the good, Mike argues that it would be a mistake to treat the very difficult as though it were impossible. He believes that the case—indeed, the imperative—for eliminating nuclear weapons is so compelling that our leaders should still work in that direction, and he lays out a plan for doing so.

In that sense, this book is a classic O'Hanlon—and Brookings—product: it identifies in a hardheaded and lucid fashion a major problem, but it also offers a bold but pragmatic solution.

Mike is grateful to a number of reviewers, formal and informal, as well as other colleagues, including Richard Betts, Barry Blechman, Richard Bush, Vanda Felbab-Brown, Martin Indyk, Steven

Pifer, Kenneth Pollack, and Peter Singer. Thanks also to Brookings Press colleagues under director Bob Faherty who moved this book forward, and especially copyeditor Marty Gottron. He also thanks Jason Campbell and Ian Livingston for research assistance and Jason Mehta for very important and helpful assistance in understanding various aspects of international treaty law.

STROBE TALBOTT
President
Brookings Institution

Washington, D.C.
July 2010

A SKEPTIC'S CASE
FOR NUCLEAR DISARMAMENT

1 THE VISION OF NUCLEAR DISARMAMENT

CAN MANKIND UNINVENT THE nuclear bomb and rid the world of the greatest military threat to the human species and the survival of the planet that has ever been created? Logic might seem to say of course not. But the president of the United States and a number of key foreign policy dignitaries are now on record as saying yes. They acknowledge that a world free of nuclear weapons remains a vision, not immediately attainable and perhaps not achievable within the lifetimes of most contemporary policymakers. But they believe that the vision needs to be made visible, vibrant, and powerful.

Since former secretaries of state George Shultz and Henry Kissinger, former defense secretary Bill Perry, and former senator Sam Nunn wrote a newspaper column in January 2007 advocating a nuclear-free world, a movement to attempt just that has been gaining in strength. Prominent scholars have lent their voices to the idea.[1] Notably, a group of one hundred signatories (not including the above four) convened in Paris in December 2008 and established Global Zero, a movement whose goal is to rid the world of nuclear weapons by 2030 through a multilateral, universal, verified process. The group wants negotiations on the global zero treaty to begin by 2019—quite possibly during the term of President Barack Obama's successor.[2]

As a "citizens' campaign," Global Zero has drawn inspiration from the recent grass-roots effort to craft a land-mine treaty and from the important work of several wealthy and influential private individuals in spearheading global antipoverty campaigns. Its goal is built on earlier work, including the 1996 report of the influential Canberra Commission on the Elimination of Nuclear Weapons.[3] Calls for eliminating the bomb are as old as the bomb itself, and there have also been bursts of energy devoted to the disarmament cause at various other moments in the past such as the early to mid-1980s.[4] But the pace of activity, including the organization of this movement, has accelerated greatly in recent years. The movement now has a serious strategy for moving forward—not at some distant time when miraculous new inventions might make nukes obsolete, but within the next ten years, when a treaty might be written, even if another ten years would be needed to put it into effect.

Will President Obama really pursue Global Zero or some other serious agenda for nuclear disarmament? Will he go beyond the inspiring speech he gave in Prague in 2009, the modest cuts in deployed forces he and the Russians agreed to in the New START Treaty, and the somewhat lowered profile of nuclear weapons set out in his April 2010 Nuclear Posture Review?[5] These steps are not insignificant, but they still leave the world very far from nuclear disarmament.[6] The much-heralded Nuclear Security Summit in April 2010 in Washington was worthwhile. But it was primarily notable not for its progress toward nuclear zero but for its promotion of actions to reduce the risks of nuclear theft, accident, and terrorism. For example, Mexico agreed to convert a research reactor from highly enriched uranium (usable in bombs) to lower-enriched uranium (not usable), Ukraine agreed to eliminate its stocks of highly enriched uranium within two years, and the United States and Russia recommitted to eliminating an excess stock of plutonium.[7] These steps, as well as the administration's request for a 25 percent increase to fund global nonproliferation activities (to $2.7 billion in the fiscal year 2011 budget), are entirely sensible.[8] But whether Obama will push nuclear issues in additional bold new ways anytime soon seems dubious—when on other national security matters such as Iraq and Afghanistan he has been extremely pragmatic and deferential to military advisers, who do not generally appear enthusiastic about nuclear disarmament, and when many other priorities beginning with promoting economic recovery compete for his time and attention.

Perhaps Obama will in effect drop the nuclear disarmament goal. But nuclear crises in Iran and North Korea, among other things, may keep it alive. As this American president realizes, the real motivation for the idea of abolishing nuclear weapons is neither utopian nor futuristic. It is not simply to deny extremist countries the excuse of getting the bomb because others already have it.[9] Rather, the motivation is to put significant pressure—more so than is possible today—on rogue countries if they pursue such weapons anyway. With leaders in Teheran, Pyongyang, and elsewhere bent on obtaining nuclear weapons, and charging U.S. policymakers with double standards in their insistence that the United States can have the bomb but they cannot, the president's ability to galvanize a global coalition to pressure Iran and North Korea (and perhaps others) into walking back their weapons programs may depend on regaining the moral high ground. And that in turn may require an American commitment to work toward giving up its own arsenal—once doing so is verifiable and once others agree to do the same.

But how to rid the world of nuclear weapons as well as bomb-ready fissile materials? And how to do so safely? Perhaps a nuclear abolition treaty could constructively contribute to global stability if done right. But it could be hazardous if done wrong. Among other things countries that currently depend on America's military protection could decide they should seek nuclear weapons of their

TABLE 1-1. Global Nuclear Weapons Inventories,
Late 2009 Estimates

Russia	13,000
United States	9,400
France	300
China	240
Britain	180
Israel	90
Pakistan	80
India	70
North Korea	8

Source: Robert S. Norris and Hans M. Kristensen, "Nuclear Notebook: Worldwide Deployments of Nuclear Weapons, 2009," *Bulletin of the Atomic Scientists* (November/ December 2009), p. 87 (www.thebulletin.org [December 2009]); and Larry A. Niksch, "North Korea's Nuclear Weapons Development and Diplomacy" (Congressional Research Service, May 27, 2009) (http://italy.usembassy.gov/pdf/other/RL33590.pdf [December 2009]).

own. If the Turkeys and Saudi Arabias and Japans and Taiwans of the world interpret the U.S. debate over nuclear disarmament to imply that they can no longer rely on the United States as a dependable strategic partner (a formal ally in the cases of Turkey and Japan, an informal but still trusted friend in the cases of Saudi Arabia and Taiwan)—because it no longer takes deterrence as seriously as before—serious consequences could result. The Global Zero movement could wind up sparking the very wave of nuclear proliferation and instability it hopes to prevent. Sam Nunn (not himself a member of the Global Zero movement because of its near-term schedule for pursuing a disarmament treaty) uses the image of nuclear disarmament as a mountain— with the summit currently beyond reach and perhaps out of sight. He advocates moving from the current position to a higher base camp (meaning much deeper disarmament and related measures) to determine if the summit can in fact be reached at some point.[10] That image makes sense—but the United States and its allies must also be safe on the way to the new base camp and avoid committing to a particular route to the top too soon.

So far, not enough advocates of the nuclear disarmament idea are addressing, or even acknowledging, such complexities and complications. Some are doing so, and I have benefited greatly from the work of scholars such as George Perkovich, Barry Blechman, Bruce Blair, Hal Feiveson, and Frank von Hippel in writing this book. Jonathan Schell's original concept from the 1980s of dismantling nuclear arms while recognizing the possible need to reconstitute them—particularly in the cold war setting about which he wrote then—also informs my vision of what a practical nuclear disarmament regime might be. But today's movement as a whole still begins with a desired destination and then tries to find ways to make it happen. My analytical approach is different—instead of working backward from a desired endpoint, it follows an empirical and deductive approach to assess the feasibility of eliminating nuclear weapons, starting with first principles of international security, modern history, and nuclear physics.

This book does not argue against the notion of nuclear abolition; it is in fact a friendly skeptic's case *for* nuclear disarmament. But I emphasize the conditions and caveats that would have to accompany any such treaty regime—including clear rules for ways the major powers might consider temporarily rearming themselves with nuclear arms in the event of a future violation of the treaty regime, even after weapons had been eliminated. The scenarios here are potentially more complex than many nuclear disarmament advocates have acknowledged to date. What if a dangerous country is suspected of having an active nuclear weapons program, and verification cannot resolve the matter? What if a country develops an advanced biological pathogen with enormous potential lethality—and perhaps even an antidote to protect its own people? Would nuclear deterrence truly be irrelevant or inappropriate as a means of addressing such a problem?

Many, if not most, advocates of nuclear disarmament consider the abolition of nuclear weapons the moral equivalent of the abolition of slavery—and imply that, just as with slavery, once eliminated, nuclear weapons should be gone for good (absent a blatant violation of the treaty by a country that chooses to build a nuclear arsenal in the future). This is a dangerous way to portray the vision of disarmament, however, for it would deprive the United States of deterrent options that may be needed someday given the unpredictable future course of human history. In other words, even once nuclear weapons are eliminated, they may not be eliminated forever. At a practical level, the world will likely have many nuclear power plants as well as all the nuclear waste that nuclear bomb and energy programs will have generated; fissile material can be gleaned from all of these sources. The knowledge to make nuclear weapons will not disappear, and relevant nuclear materials will not do so either.

What of the issue of timing—not only of when to try to negotiate and then implement a treaty but how to describe the vision of nuclear disarmament in the short term? Many nuclear disarmament advocates pull back the minute anyone asks if they want a treaty soon, recognizing the impracticality of trying to abolish nuclear weapons in the next few years. But they are the ones who elevated the idea in the contemporary nuclear debate to a level not seen for many decades, so putting off the timing issue is neither consistent nor advisable. In fact, there are good reasons to have this debate now. Eliminating nuclear weapons from the face of the Earth has technically been a goal of U.S. policy since the 1960s, for example. Moreover, the slowness of negotiating the recent New START Treaty with Moscow and the likely slow ratification debates over both it and the Comprehensive Nuclear Test Ban Treaty in the coming years suggest the possibility that nuclear debates will bog down in technicalities and mundane practicalities, losing sight of the big picture. So bold ideas are useful to provoke fresh thinking and serious action. That said, the ideas of nuclear disarmament advocates are already raising questions around the world about how long the American extended deterrent can be depended upon to help ensure regional peace in key theaters. The resulting perceptions can in turn affect countries' decisions about whether to pursue their own bombs—not only extremist nations but even friendly states that worry they may no longer be able to depend on the United States.

I argue for a middle-ground position. Moving to nuclear disarmament soon by trying to write a treaty in the next few years is too fast. But dropping the subject for now and waiting for the twenty-second century or some other distant date is too slow.

In addition to possibly spooking U.S. allies who worry about how they will ensure their security in a dangerous world, there are two problems with trying to abolish nuclear weapons too soon. Deterrent arrangements that are working today, but that are also somewhat fragile, could be disrupted; and states entirely disinterested in nuclear disarmament might be encouraged to build up arsenals in the hope that their nascent nuclear power might be greater as the existing nuclear powers build down. The main problem, though, is that the nuclear disarmament notion simply lacks credibility in a world in which even some existing nuclear powers clearly have no interest in denuclearizing anytime soon (even if the United States did). Absent a serious process for moving toward zero, declaration of ambitious but arbitrary and unattainable deadlines for action is more likely in the end to discredit the initiative than to advance it.

The problem with putting off debate about nuclear disarmament, however, is that existing powers remain in a weak position to pressure would-be proliferators to abstain from the pursuit of nuclear weapons. Procrastination also perpetuates a false sense of complacency about the supposed safety of living with the bomb. What is needed is a prudent form of urgency. Neither haste and impetuousness nor indefinite postponement of the issue will do.

The United States should endorse a nuclear-free world with conviction, as President Obama did in his 2009 Prague speech. But it should not work to create a treaty now and should not sign any treaty that others might create for the foreseeable future. The right time horizon for seriously pushing a new nuclear accord is when most of the world's half dozen or so major territorial and existential issues involving major powers are resolved—and this cannot be set to a calendar as precisely as the Global Zero movement would like. Discussed further below, these issues include the status of Taiwan, the issue of Kashmir, political relations between Russia and the key "near-abroad" states of Georgia and Ukraine, and the state of Israel. Nuclear crises involving Iran and North Korea also need to be addressed, although the beginnings of a move toward nuclear disarmament might not have to await their complete resolution. Once these contentious matters are largely resolved, the plausibility of great-power war over any imaginable issue that one can identify today will be very low. That will in turn make the basic structure and functioning of the international political system stable enough to risk moving toward a nuclear-free world—a process so radical as to be inherently destabilizing in some sense and thus prudent to pursue only when the great powers are in a cooperative mode and undivided by irredentist territorial issues.

Some will argue that there is no foreseeable period of great-power peace and thus no prospect of the preconditions required for moving to a denuclearized world. They believe for the most part that the prospects of great-power war in the future will be as, or nearly as, great as they were in prenuclear eras of human history. Such individuals often call themselves realists and imply that ideas such as nuclear disarmament are just too utopian to be within mankind's reach. But as argued below, this so-called realist argument is also problematic—the history of fallible mankind, and particularly of the nuclear age to date, makes it hard to believe that nuclear weapons will never be used if they continue to occupy a central role in international politics. If realism means that nuclear war likely will occur someday, how can such a worldview be called prudent—indeed, how can it even be called realist, with all the connotations of pragmatism that the term implies?

That said, my vision for nuclear disarmament is one of dismantling nuclear warheads—a vision that should not be confused with their permanent abolition, a term favored by some. The desire to eliminate such weapons forever is understandable, given their incredible destructive power; most plausible uses of nuclear weapons would in fact be inhumane and illegitimate. But it is war itself that is most inhumane, and war targeting civilians through whatever means is the fundamental moral blight we should be trying to eliminate. Certain forms of highly lethal biological weapons attack with advanced pathogens, large-scale conventional conflict resembling the world wars, and wars that include genocide could be every bit as inhumane as a nuclear attack. Outlawing nuclear weapons in a way that increases the prospects of other types of immoral warfare would be no accomplishment at all. Therefore, even as the international community strives to dismantle nuclear weapons, it needs practical options for rebuilding them should other perils present themselves—not only suspected pursuit of nuclear arms by a country bent on violating the accord but perhaps also the development of advanced biological pathogens (a threat the Obama administration's 2010 Nuclear Posture Review considers[11]) or an especially threatening conventional military buildup by a future extremist state. That is the broad, strategic argument in favor of preserving options for reconstitution, even after a nuclear disarmament treaty is signed and implemented.

Any disarmament treaty must therefore allow a country like the United States the right of temporary withdrawal from the treaty not only for obvious nuclear weapons violations by a threatening state, but even for suspected nuclear weapons violations—as well as for advanced biological pathogen programs and extremely threatening conventional military buildups by a major power. This list of exemptions is far longer than most nuclear zero proponents favor or are even willing to countenance. But the nature of international relations, and of modern weaponry, leave little choice in the matter. The terms by which the right of temporary withdrawal could be exercised must be stated as clearly as possible, and a burden of proof must be placed on any state or group of states exercising the right. Giving the UN Security Council the ultimate say in whether temporary nuclear weapons reconstitution is allowable would not be a sound idea, but the council should have an opportunity to hear the argument of a country that believes it must rearm in response to the belligerent actions of another. In addition, a contact group of states with varying political perspectives should be created, able to hear and discuss sensitive intelligence, for each country that might someday consider the option of rearming. The contact group would not have veto power either, but it would be able to offer independent assessments on whether a defensive form of rearmament was warranted. For the United States, such a group might include not only traditional close allies but countries like Brazil and India.

Capricious or blatantly self-serving reconstitution must be avoided. But a nuclear disarmament treaty that precluded the international community from responding to the actions of an advanced military power strongly suspected of pursuing nuclear, biological, or enormous conventional military capabilities would be a chimera. The terms of such a treaty would not withstand the stresses that the real world might place upon it, should such a threatening state challenge the global order at some future point. In other words, such a treaty would be violated by countries faced with acute threats to their own security. A treaty that possesses such inherent contradictions should not be drafted.

There is also a technical reason to view reconstitution as a real future policy option, even short of circumstances in which another country has egregiously violated the accord by building up a new nuclear arsenal. Simply put, nuclear weapons will always be within reach of mankind in the future, whatever we may do, whatever we may prefer. Even as they improve, verification methods will almost surely not be capable of fully ensuring that all existing materials are dismantled or destroyed. The laws of physics make it very hard to be certain that all bombs and bomb-grade materials had been eliminated in all parts of the world. Even more so, the future of the nuclear power industry makes it very likely that bomb-grade materials will be salvageable from nuclear fuel or nuclear waste within months of a decision to do so. In other words, not only is permanent, irreversible abolition unwise, it is also probably impossible. But dismantlement of all existing bomb and fissile material inventories, in recognition of the fact that the day-to-day role of nuclear weapons in international security is dangerous and ultimately unsustainable, should become the goal, as President Obama has rightly emphasized.

Some might argue that with all these caveats and conditions, a nuclear disarmament treaty, even one that is patiently and prudently pursued, is not worth the trouble. They underestimate both the danger posed by nuclear weapons and the positive power of ideas and ideals in international politics. These weapons are so heinously destructive as to be illegitimate; they are indiscriminate killers, and they have proven to be far harder to build and handle safely than many understand. Even more harm could be caused today by moving precipitously to eliminate them than by keeping them. That said, nuclear weapons have no proper role even as visible deterrents in the normal interactions of states, and the United States should aspire to a world—and try to create a world—in which they would no longer have such an active, operational role.

The Motivation of the Abolition Movement

Twenty years after the cold war ended, those favoring the elimination of nuclear weapons often point to four main motivations.

First, the weapons are simply inhumane. They kill indiscriminately and are immensely destructive, leaving them no proper place in the national security policies or armed forces establishments of respectable countries. If conventional weapons such as napalm, carpet bombing, and incendiary weapons are no longer used because they are considered immoral, then a type of weaponry with hundreds of times the lethality should not have any legitimate place in a country's military arsenal either.

Second, the basic logic of the Non-Proliferation Treaty (NPT) seems unsustainable. The NPT was built on double standards—those that apply to the nuclear haves, and those that apply to the have-nots. But when negotiated in the 1960s, during a period of intense cold war arms racing, the idea that the United States and the Soviet Union would disarm was unrealistic. The only realistic goal for the superpowers seemed to be that they curb their nuclear competition. So the NPT was in that sense a practical response to the world in which it was negotiated. With the cold war over, the logical inconsistency, and political unfairness, of an NPT regime in which some countries are allowed nuclear weapons in perpetuity while others are denied them categorically seems increasingly unsustainable.

The NPT itself also calls for an end to these double standards—specifically, Article VI calls for "general and complete disarmament." That reads like utopianism to many, because the language implies an end to all organized military forces, not just nuclear abolition.[12] But the NPT review conference of 2000 reaffirmed the nuclear aspect of the goal, making disarmament simply impractical to ignore, since it is now part of the bargain that commits most states not to pursue their own nuclear arms.[13]

Third, abolitionists argue that "loose nukes" remain a serious worry. During the cold war, when the states possessing nuclear weapons were few in number and typically strong in their internal controls, this worry was not so great. But with at least nine nuclear powers today, three or four of them subject to possible internal strife, the danger of theft or confiscation is very high. We should not hyperventilate over the imminence of the threat, as academic John Mueller has rightly pointed out.[14] But to trivialize the destructive force of these weapons, or to assume that no nuclear accident or other disaster will happen in the future because one has not happened in half a century, would be to make a major mistake in the opposite direction of complacency, as the next chapter will argue. The dangers seem destined to keep growing as the nuclear club possibly expands further—a development that may accelerate with the world's renewed interest in nuclear power, since preparation of nuclear fuel inherently involves many of the same technologies that are used to produce fissile materials for weapons. We should consider ourselves lucky that a loose nuclear weapon or mass of plutonium or enriched uranium has not harmed anyone yet, rather than grow complacent.

Fourth, the domestic politics of this "big idea" could be transformative in engaging the public on the issue, at least in theory. Tired of incrementalism, the American public has long since lost its real interest in arms control. So has much of the rest of the world. As a result, when accords such as the Comprehensive Test Ban Treaty come up for Senate ratification, there is little popular engagement and treaty opponents can carry the day. Only a revolutionary proposal can break this logjam and lead to a true national debate in which obstructionist forces can be challenged and defeated—or so the argument might go. A similar logic may apply to the internal politics of numerous other nuclear nations.

Counterarguments

All of these abolitionist arguments have some merit. But there are also strong counterarguments that raise the stakes in the debate to a very high level. In short, we may not be able to live safely with nuclear weapons, yet it is not clear how we could live safely without them.

Much of the cold war nuclear literature is filled with discussions of "extended deterrence"—devising credible ways for a nuclear power like the United States to persuade would-be aggressors not to attack its allies. Nuclear weapons had a large role in this debate when the possible enemy was a hypermilitarized Soviet Union abutting key American allies. As Keith Payne points out, in addition to deterring would-be aggressors, American security commitments must also provide positive *assurance* to friends and allies. That is especially critical when the goal is prevention of nuclear proliferation, since nervous allies may elect to build their own nuclear arsenals to feel comfortable with their own security circumstances.

Perhaps the tasks of both extended deterrence and assurance are easier now that the Soviet Union is gone. And in many ways these tasks surely are easier for the United States and a large number of its allies. But Russia may feel an even greater need for nuclear weapons now than it did during the cold war, given Western conventional military superiority.[15] This is a complicating matter in any pursuit of nuclear disarmament, because without the support of other powers for the idea, there can be no worldwide elimination of nuclear weapons.

And even the United States and its allies face complications in this more complex period of multiple nuclear powers that some have called the "second nuclear age."[16] To take one example, is Japan really confident it will never need nuclear weapons to deter a rising China? And if Japan gains nuclear weapons, what will South Korea, then surrounded by four nuclear weapons states, choose to do? Worst of all, perhaps, will Taiwan really believe that an already-indirect American security pledge is reliable enough that it can forgo a nuclear capability of its own? Since China has in the past declared that Taiwanese pursuit of nuclear weapons would be grounds for war, this scenario is very troublesome.

The situation is also very difficult in the Middle East. To be sure, Iran is attempting to justify its own nuclear programs by exploiting the alleged hypocrisy of the NPT regime and the established nuclear powers. Depriving Teheran of this excuse for its nuclear ambitions would seem to argue in favor of a nuclear abolition treaty. But few countries really seem swayed by Teheran's arguments. Rather, their commercial interests in Iran, or their inherent belief in positive diplomacy as a tool for improving other states' behavior, or even a desire to frustrate the United States seem to be more important factors limiting their willingness to get tough with the Iranian regime. The world's acute need for Iran's oil further compounds the problem. It is not clear that the double standards of the NPT are the core of the problem.

Iran has made direct and grave threats against Israel in recent years. It has also thrown its weight around quite a bit in the region, in Iraq, Lebanon, and the Persian Gulf, to the point of threatening the stability of ruling regimes. Under such circumstances, American steps toward nuclear disarmament could produce undesired dynamics. Countries like Saudi Arabia that do not have formal security alliances with the United States could be extremely skittish about facing an Iranian nuclear capability without their own deterrent, should Washington join other key capitals in moving toward a nuclear-free world. They may fear that Iran would cheat even after signing such a treaty. Teheran might then try to intimidate its neighbors, who could worry that Iran possessed the bomb even after the United States had deprived itself of its own arsenal. In addition, reports continue to appear now and again of possible arrangements under which Pakistan would provide Saudi Arabia with nuclear weapons in a crisis situation if need be.[17] In recent work at Brookings, Martin Indyk and others have suggested that in response to Iran's apparent ambitions, the United States might need to *increase* rather than diminish the robustness of its nuclear guarantees to key regional friends if it is to discourage them from acquiring nuclear weapons of their own.

Some argue that, with the cold war over and American military preponderance so clear to all, nuclear umbrellas are no longer needed to ensure deterrence. Overwhelming conventional military superiority can suffice, they say—even if an adversary might itself have chemical or biological arms or a secret nuclear bomb program. But this argument is facile. Conventional military dominance is harder to attain, and sustain, than many acknowledge; in many cases translating that dominance into rapid and decisive victories can be equally difficult. In the aftermath of the Iraq and Afghanistan wars, it is impossible to know just how willing Americans will be to use force to defend far-away allies—especially if adversaries might use or threaten to use weapons of mass destruction. And as I have argued, along with others, for years, trends in military technology are not making the task of deploying decisive military force to distant regions radically easier. Even classic defensive missions can be hard to conduct with conventional arms alone. In other words, situations like the Iraqi invasion of Kuwait in 1990 or Serbian attacks on Kosovar Albanians in 1999 cannot be confidently prevented, and rolling back such aggressions, especially by a more advanced state, can be hard. Of course, nuclear deterrence will often be of dubious relevance to such scenarios too, but it may be helpful in certain egregious cases; the possibility cannot be dismissed.[18]

Some also hope that missile defenses may improve enough that offensive nuclear weapons will fade in significance, and defenses become dominant, in many key regions of the world. Yes, missile defense can lower the odds of successful attack, especially by lesser powers with small missile arsenals of limited sophistication. But a reliable missile defense against advanced threats has yet to be built. If the day ever arrives when such a defense is possible, it will be far into the future. Currently, missile defenses would do very well to intercept a few warheads launched without advanced countermeasures from a predictable location. Larger attacks, surprise attacks, and sophisticated attacks will probably be capable of punching through available defenses for a very long time to come.

Then there is the problem of verification. Nuclear arms control agreements to date have limited large objects, such as intercontinental ballistic missile silos and heavy bombers; the agreements have indirectly constrained missile warheads, air-launched cruise missiles, and the like by counting the launchers that carry them. The world today is full of additional bombs, a great deal of additional bomb material, and nuclear waste and energy facilities in dozens of countries that contain materials that could be diverted to weapons purposes. Sometimes the country holding relevant material does not know the exact amounts in its possession. Fissile materials can be shielded well enough that their physical emissions are apparent only to detectors within a few dozens of meters of their locations. In other words, their characteristic signatures are not easily noticed, making verification that they have been eliminated difficult if not impossible. Even centrifuge facilities and other possible technologies for uranium enrichment can be rather well hidden. Arms control protocols allowing inspections of suspected sites can help—but they work only if outsiders can articulate their suspicions with enough precision to allow inspectors to target the right locations. This usually requires having defectors or spies inside a country who are able to develop initial leads on illicit programs. Gaining such tip-offs in timely fashion cannot be taken for granted. Some argue that in the future, changes in global morality will make it much more likely that "societal verification" could unearth a bomb program from within a state bent on cheating. This assumption would seem optimistic given the long history of extremist states being able to convince or coerce their own citizens to remain silent even in the face of enormous atrocities committed by governments against their own people or their neighbors.

Biological pathogens are another complicating matter. If a modified form of smallpox, perhaps genetically joined with a very contagious influenza-like organism, could be developed and then employed against populations, millions could die. The attacking country, knowing more about the properties of the pathogen it had developed than anyone else, might be able to inoculate its own citizens against the disease in advance. Perhaps even more plausibly, it might claim it had such an antidote and then threaten to unleash the biological agent on other countries if they did not accede to its demands of one type or another. How could such attacks—or perhaps other types of mass casualty attacks that currently cannot be foreseen—be deterred absent nuclear weapons? A conventional response requiring many months of preparation and combat could be tough to execute if many of the soldiers of the retaliating country were falling ill from a disease that their doctors were powerless to prevent or to cure.

A Realistic Path to Zero—And a Realistic Definition of Zero

In the end the arguments both for and against nuclear disarmament are extremely strong. How to resolve them?

First, a word on timing. The world is not ready to take even the initial steps toward negotiating a nuclear disarmament treaty. It will not be ready until great-power peace is more firmly established, necessitating progress on key issues in East Asia, South Asia, the Middle East, and eastern Europe. These matters cannot be set to a calendar, so current aspirations for developing even a notional timeline for pursuing a binding global zero accord are unwarranted. In fact, they are potentially harmful because they convey the sense that somehow the great powers (or some of them) have made nuclear weapons abolition a higher priority than the preservation of great-power peace. That would be a major strategic mistake.

Looking further down the road, this book supports the nuclear disarmament agenda—but only by recasting it. Rather than think of an absolute end state, in which nuclear weapons are abolished forever, treaty proponents will have to be more realistic. They will have to settle for a world in which all nuclear weapons are in fact disassembled and destroyed—but in which the ability to rebuild a modest arsenal fairly quickly is preserved technically, politically, and legally. Such an arsenal would be built only in an extreme situation. Ideally, such a reconstitution option would never be invoked, but it is critical that the option be retained. Nuclear zero should not amount simply to de-alerting or disassembly of weapons, with stocks of fissile materials at the ready (above and beyond those modest amounts of materials that could be quickly available through the nuclear energy fuel cycle). A world of weapons-grade and bomb-ready highly enriched uranium and plutonium, maintained in significant quantities, would retain nuclear weapons too close to the center of international military planning and global power relationships.[19] But a nuclear disarmament accord should generally permit what cannot be banned verifiably. As such, *plans* for reconstitution should be fairly robust even if facilities and materials for rebuilding arsenals should not be. Given that the existence of nuclear power plants will give many governments the option of building arsenals within months, even if highly enriched uranium can be eliminated as a fuel and even if plutonium reprocessing is stopped, these plans should be fairly "warm."

Ruling out the option of reconstitution claims more knowledge about the future than anyone can have. Some proponents of eliminating the bomb recognize this, but others do not, and in most cases the mechanisms of planning for reconstitution are not given adequate thought. In fact, a central element of any nuclear disarmament regime must be a way to end or at least suspend that regime—in diplomatic, legal, military, and technical terms.

Hoping otherwise, and assuming that eliminating nuclear weapons by treaty means abolishing them forever, presupposes a favorable international security environment among the great powers that may not endure permanently. It therefore runs too high a risk of driving security-conscious states to build nuclear arsenals themselves. It risks worsening the very proliferation problem that the disarmament goal is designed largely to address.

Perhaps the world can get rid of nuclear weapons—as long as it knows that it can rebuild them in the event of a sufficiently grave violation of the regime by an aggressive country. Under such circumstances, the world will need legal and physical mechanisms for deciding whether to rebuild a nuclear capability to punish a regime violator. Not only the obvious case of a violating state building nuclear weapons but also other possible actions need to be woven into the framework. High suspicion that an aggressive state is building a bomb may suffice to justify others rearming, at least temporarily, even without hard evidence or irrefutable proof. Extremely lethal biological pathogens in the hands of a ruthless regime may also legitimate reconstitution of another country's arsenal, depending on circumstances, as described in chapter 3. Indeed, genocide carried out with conventional weapons may itself be reason enough.[20]

The Manhattan Project was clearly motivated largely by American fears about Germany's bomb program. But replaying the events of World War II in one's imagination, it is hard to argue that the United States should have eschewed nuclear weapons even if it knew full well that Nazi Germany and Imperial Japan could not get them. One can admittedly still debate whether the United States should have used its nuclear weapons, but the argument that it should have made denuclearization a higher priority than ending a war that killed more than 50 million people is far from persuasive.

As subsequent chapters explain, a nuclear disarmed world requires a strategy for reconstitution *before* a treaty is even pursued, to avoid possibly pernicious and counterproductive dynamics as the treaty is negotiated and implemented. From an American perspective, this includes:

—Specific clauses in the treaty allowing reconstitution in the event of a direct violation of the treaty by another party (this provision is probably already a given).

—More controversially, clauses allowing nuclear reconstitution in the event of development of a particularly lethal advanced biological pathogen or other highly threatening weapon (even including a sufficiently extreme conventional military buildup).

—Clauses allowing a government to bring intelligence information to the UN Security Council if it fears that another government is violating the treaty and wants to respond quickly. In other words, there must be a mechanism for debating violations *before* they culminate in actual production or deployment or use of a bomb.

—A U.S. capacity, including access to facilities at a place such as Los Alamos National Laboratory (and other sites, in case the main site is attacked preemptively), to reconstitute a team of nuclear weapons experts capable of rebuilding a modest number of warheads within months of a decision to do so. Other countries may of course choose to exercise a similar right.

—An American statement to the effect that even if the UN Security Council rejects an argument that another country is believed to be building nuclear or advanced biological agents, the United States reserves the right under Article 51 of the UN Charter to rebuild a nuclear arsenal anyway, once a contact group of countries had been familiarized with the U.S. case for reconstitution and allowed to comment publicly. This right would have to be invoked only in a truly extreme case, should be temporary in its application—and ideally would never be needed. But absent such a statement, America's role as a guarantor of the security of many other countries would be at risk, and the incentives for others to build their own weapons would increase undesirably. Once again, the proliferation costs could easily outweigh the benefits; more states rather than fewer might wind up with the bomb.

The book concludes with discussion of the near-term nuclear policy agenda. Nuclear disarmament will take a long time to achieve under the best of circumstances. To ensure that the nuclear disarmament agenda does not become as irrelevant to near-term policymaking, and ultimately as utopian in character, as Article VI of the Non-Proliferation Treaty, therefore, we must look for ways for it to influence the current policy agenda at least modestly. In fact, there are ways to do so. These include the more rapid elimination of excess warheads than some might favor, greater efforts to develop inspection and verification concepts for warheads as well as fissile materials, and a continued effort by the United States to design ballistic missile defense systems that other major powers find generally nonthreatening.

2 THE CASE FOR ELIMINATING NUCLEAR WEAPONS

THE CASE FOR ELIMINATING nuclear weapons from the face of the Earth begins with the simple and compelling argument that humankind has ultimately used every type of weapon it has ever created. While we cannot uninvent nuclear weapons, we can attempt to remove them from the planet. If we do not, it seems almost certain they will again be used someday—perhaps with far more devastating effect than the Hiroshima and Nagasaki bombings in 1945. A modest-sized bomb could kill 100,000 people or more, and each thermonuclear weapon (commonly known as a hydrogen bomb) could destroy ten times that many. Worse, if several bombs of whatever size were detonated, the cumulative effects would likely be multiplicative. Hospitals would be overwhelmed (unlike the 9/11 attacks, where most victims were killed, many people would be severely and acutely injured); infrastructure would be destroyed, leaving millions if not tens of millions without shelter, heat, electricity, water, or dependable food supplies; and many leaders from government, business, and other crucial sectors of society would likely be lost. Attacks involving dozens of weapons could kill many, many millions of people and leave societal chaos in their wake for years if not decades.

Indeed, it is worth pausing a moment to consider several lessons of the atomic bombings of Japan that helped end World War II. President Harry Truman ordered these extremely lethal and indiscriminate attacks—and has nonetheless been largely lionized by history as a great leader. The attacks were carried out when the outcome of World War II was hardly in doubt; the issue was how to save perhaps hundreds of thousands of American lives by avoiding a possible invasion of Japan, accelerate an end to the war, and minimize the Soviet role in the Far East in the postwar environment. While these stakes were hardly insignificant, they did not involve the basic survival of the United States and its main allies. Yet nuclear weapons were used, and used in a manner that relatively few Americans challenged—either at the time or later.[1] This is a sobering indication of the way in which a nation at war could decide—in fact, did decide—to use the most powerful weapon on Earth against men, women, and children alike rather than prolong a conventional fight that it was virtually sure to win. If a democracy like the United States, which emphasizes human rights, could use nuclear weapons, why would anyone believe that any other country faced with high military stakes in the future, and uncertain of winning short of a nuclear attack, would hesitate to do so?

The above argument is intended not to impugn Truman but only to remind those who consider use of nuclear weapons somehow unthinkable that in fact they have been used by a great country, with a respected president making the decision to bomb. Some opponents of nuclear weapons consider their use a violation of international law and even a crime against humanity on a par with genocide, given the indiscriminate and highly lethal nature of the technology.[2] Debating these issues is not my purpose here. Rather, the point is that nuclear weapons *are* usable, they have been used, and they could be used again.

The World War II experience offers a second lesson that is directly relevant to discussions of nuclear disarmament. While demonstrating the dangers of nuclear weapons, that experience should also instill a pragmatism about the prospects for permanently banning the bomb. It strikes me as axiomatic that were another threat like that posed by Hitler or Stalin to arise even *after* a nuclear disarmament treaty of some kind had been negotiated and implemented, peaceful nations would preemptively reconstitute nuclear capabilities whether or not they had evidence that the feared aggressor state or states were themselves doing so. They would not wait for proof. At that point, prudence would require them to be sure that they were not left without the bomb. Among other things, they would have to calculate that any state with an extremist ideology, claims on neighbors' territory, and a major military buildup under way would probably not hesitate to build nuclear weapons as well. Even if the extremist regime did not build the bomb, there is little reason to think that the status quo powers should forgo such capabilities, were the looming threat to appear great enough. This is a point to which I return in chapter 4, where the nature of any nuclear disarmament treaty is explored, including the circumstances under which states would have the right of temporary withdrawal from treaty obligations.

Most of today's nuclear disarmament proponents would not accept my argument, believing that the only purpose of nuclear weapons should be to deter the development, threatened use, and actual use of nuclear arms. I do not believe this position comports with the realities of international politics—or at least with possible future developments in international politics. The chances of a future threat of such magnitude developing will, I believe, be quite modest in the future. But the future is very long span of time, and it is uncertain. Hedging options are needed.

So the history of World War II holds a complex, mixed message for the nuclear disarmament agenda. But aside from the World War II experience, the case for moving with all possible haste to a nuclear-free world can be reinforced with several straightforward arguments. They add up to a powerful indictment of the notion that we can survive a world with a significant number of nuclear powers over an indefinite period of time without the weapons actually being employed. These factors include:

—The history of the nuclear age, beginning with World War II but focusing particularly on several key cold war crises, as well as Indo-Pakistani crises of the recent past. These cases strongly suggest that nuclear war between rival states or countries engaged in war is indeed possible. The number of such states with nuclear weapons is of course continuing to grow, a foreboding development.

—The technical dangers of operating nuclear weapons safely, including the risks of accident in peacetime and malfunctioning command and control in crisis or war.

—The dangers of proliferation of nuclear weapons to a growing number of countries and the related dangers of nuclear terrorism—combined with the modern phenomenon of terrorist movements bent on causing massive destruction.

The Risks of War

There is an ongoing and legitimate debate about how close the world has come to nuclear war since 1945. But the debate is over the magnitude of the risk, not its existence. In fact, it would be folly to think that having collectively invested trillions of dollars in nuclear weapons since their invention, nation states would not seek some benefit, up to and including the threat of using the weapons. And the nature of human beings and governments means that such threats are not always well managed or controlled.

More than twenty years have now passed since the Berlin Wall came down and the cold war ended. Since that time, the world has been challenging enough to manage that some have become nostalgic for the cold war. Given today's problems—al Qaeda and related extremist movements; a new wave of nuclear proliferation among problematic countries such as Pakistan, North Korea, and probably Iran; and growing worries about global warming and related environmental problems—some long for the simpler days of old, when handling the world's major challenges revolved primarily around Washington, Moscow, and the U.S.-led alliance systems designed to counter the Soviet bloc.

Some also argue that nuclear weapons helped stabilize the post–World War II world.[3] There is probably some logic to this argument, and it does counsel caution in trying to move to global zero before great-power relations have been further stabilized, a point correctly emphasized by scholars like Barry Blechman and to which I return in subsequent chapters. (Memories of the extreme lethality of the world wars also contributed importantly to the subsequent absence of great-power war, as John Mueller and others have argued.) But even if nuclear weapons helped keep the peace, that hardly means that the threat of nuclear war has been safely small or that one should happily assume that nuclear deterrence can help keep the peace at acceptable risk in the future.

Nostalgia for the cold war makes little sense on multiple grounds. In fact, the cold war was a dangerous time—carrying death and destruction from the Horn of Africa to southern Africa to South and Southeast Asia to Central America. The combustible mix of decolonization, communism, and superpower proxy war intensified many conflicts and created far more violence on average than has characterized the world since. Even more to the point, for purposes of this discussion, it was a dangerous period between the great powers. Numerous crises, including several nuclear scares, brought the superpowers close to direct clashes with each other. That the United States and Soviet Union did not go to war was not a predetermined result based on their inherent prudence, the structure of their relationship, the existence of nuclear weapons, or any other such simple and decisive factor. It was, in part at least, a result of good judgments and key choices that could have gone in other directions. Fortunately, the cold war is over; whether the world would have safely survived several more decades of it is not obvious.

The point here is that major-power relationships built in part on the expectation that nuclear deterrence will keep the peace depend on optimistic interpretations of the past. In fact, there were a number of close calls, despite the supposedly stabilizing effects of extremely deadly arms in the hands of the potential belligerents.

A tradition of nonuse of nuclear weapons did in fact develop. In addition, some nuclear weapons states have over the years pledged to nonnuclear states that they will not be the subjects of nuclear attack under normal circumstances. But the tradition of nonuse, while real, is fragile. An informal norm against the employment of nuclear weapons is no guarantee that they will never be used again.[4]

The Cuban missile crisis is the lead exhibit in the history of superpower nuclear brinkmanship. In October 1962 the United States discovered Soviet missiles in Cuba capable of reaching the United States—missiles for which, it was later learned, nuclear warheads were prestationed on the island, ready for rapid mating with their delivery vehicles. A major crisis ensued when President John F. Kennedy decided that the situation was unacceptable. His efforts to compel the Soviets to remove the missiles created two of the tensest weeks in the history of the planet. Various participants estimated the odds of an actual use of nuclear weapons quite differently—Kennedy himself placed the odds at up to 1 in 2, while Kennedy's national security advisor McGeorge Bundy put them at 1 in 100. Whatever the level, virtually everyone involved agreed that the odds were too high for comfort.[5]

Bundy himself drew broad lessons from the crisis: "Recognition that the level of nuclear danger reached in October 1962 was unacceptably high for all mankind may be the most important single legacy of the Cuban missile crisis." He then continued with an assessment about the United States and Soviet Union that should be sobering to contemplate in a world with many newer, less experienced nuclear powers—many with significant territorial disputes and other major issues that divide them and produce the risk of conflict: "Having come so close to the edge, the leaders of the two governments have since taken care to keep away from the cliff." If this became true of Moscow and Washington only after living through experiences like the Cuban missile crisis, how confident can we be that other nuclear powers will act in restrained, stabilizing ways early in their own respective periods of nuclear weapons status?[6]

Michael Dobbs, in his recent account of the crisis based on archival materials that have become available in the past few years, reaches another conclusion with sobering implications as one looks to the future:

> Had someone else been president in October, 1962, the outcome could have been very different. Bobby Kennedy would later note that the dozen senior advisors who took part in the ExComm [Executive Committee] debates were all "bright and energetic. . . . amongst the most able people in the country." Nevertheless, in RFK's view, "if any of half a dozen of them were president, the world would have been very likely plunged in a catastrophic war." He based that conclusion on the knowledge that nearly half the ExComm had favored bombing the missile sites on Cuba, a step that probably would have led to an American invasion of the island.[7]

U.S. military leaders also favored a follow-on invasion that could easily have led to the use of tactical nuclear weapons by Soviet commanders on the ground.[8] Again, if one imagines a comparable scenario in the future with different leaders, whether involving the United States or not, this interpretation implies that one should not be too confident about the likelihood of a peaceful resolution.

The Cuban missile crisis was not the only scary moment involving the veiled or actual threat of nuclear weapons use during the cold war. In his seminal work about the effects of nuclear superiority (or lack thereof) on the outcome of key crises, Richard Betts identifies six "lower-risk cases" or sets of cases (Berlin 1948, the Korean War, Asian crises including Taiwan in 1954–55, Suez in 1956, Lebanon plus Taiwan in 1958, and Soviet-Chinese border clashes in 1969), as well as five higher-risk cases (Berlin 1958–59, Berlin 1961, Cuba 1962, the Middle East War of 1973, and President Jimmy Carter's response to the 1979 Soviet invasion of Afghanistan). The 1969 Soviet-Chinese border conflict did not directly involve the United States. But the period from the late 1940s through 1980 still generated on average about three events a decade.[9] And even some of the lower-risk cases on Betts's list were sobering. President Eisenhower's secretary of state John Foster Dulles was more than willing to sprinkle speeches with insinuations about possible nuclear use during the Korean War, for example. Military doctrine of the day, notably Eisenhower's New Look strategy, sought to extract maximum benefit from nuclear weapons not only as a deterrent but as a war-fighting instrument.[10]

The Berlin crisis of 1961, precipitated by Soviet threats to effectively cut off access roads to West Berlin, merits additional discussion here. Ultimately Soviet and American tanks wound up in a direct standoff, and many nuclear-related threats, some more direct than others, were made on both sides. Premier Nikita Khrushchev did not directly suggest a Soviet nuclear attack; he was thinking of having East Germans shut down access highways used by the West instead. But he was willing to challenge the United States, and any other countries who might have thought they would be protected by the U.S. nuclear advantage, by noting that Soviet nuclear upgrades had denied Washington that type of power. In effect, he was arguing that he could carry out a second strike against any U.S. first strike, thus making the threat of such a strike less likely.[11] Kennedy tended to avoid specific comments on the subject, but several in his administration hinted at nuclear possibilities, and Kennedy seems to have contemplated his preemptive nuclear strike options.[12] Secretary of Defense Robert

small-scale issues but for matters of major national interest or survival as well. Robert Jervis makes a similar point, noting that "people who believe that a situation is intolerable feel strong psychological pressures to conclude that it can be changed. Thus nuclear weapons by themselves—and even mutual second-strike capability—might not be sufficient to produce peace."[15] In other words, leaders who feel desperate may take big gambles, threatening or even using nuclear weapons, if they can convince themselves that doing so offers at least some hope of producing an acceptable outcome to a severe crisis that they cannot discern a means of exiting in any other way.

The nuclear escalation ladder, to use Herman Kahn's concept, has many rungs on it. Threatening the use of nuclear weapons, even to present limited use against discrete military targets, may therefore seem plausible options distinguishable from the unacceptable possibility of all-out nuclear war. A country determined to prevail in a given confrontation—or frustrated with its current situation and fatalistic about the status quo—can always convince itself (perhaps wrongly) that the next step will not in fact lead to the inevitability of major nuclear warfare.[16] Because some types of nuclear threats or even limited employment of nuclear weapons, in Thomas Schelling's words, "leave something to chance," they can appeal to leaders who believe that they will otherwise suffer defeat and perhaps loss of power (including possible loss of their own lives) in a given crisis or war.[17] Restraint is not a predetermined outcome because one cannot precisely predict how human beings will perform in various hypothetical circumstances. To quote another great nuclear theorist, Bernard Brodie, writing in the late 1950s regarding the possibility of a nuclear war, "the chances of its occurring are finite and perhaps even substantial, the more so as we ignore them. One almost blushes to have to make such seemingly trite statements; but we are daily bombarded with indications, in the words and acts of high officials among others, that the points have simply not sunk home."[18]

The United States and Soviet Union were not the only nuclear powers to have hair-raising encounters in recent decades. A notable case was the 1969 Soviet-Chinese border clash already mentioned. Another was the 1973 Arab-Israeli War. The Israeli government on the whole probably never came close to considering the use of nuclear weapons in light of U.S. military logistics help and a successful effort in defeating the Arab attack before Israel proper was threatened. But Chief of Army Staff Moshe Dayan reportedly believed that nuclear retaliation might well be needed and accordingly favored preparing for such a response.[19]

Another striking case was the 1999 Kargil crisis. Kargil is a small town in Indian-occupied Kashmir, five miles over the so-called line of control separating areas controlled by Pakistan from those controlled by India in this disputed province. In 1999, perhaps emboldened by its nuclear tests of the previous year that demonstrated a real weapons capability, Pakistan seized Indian military positions (temporarily deserted during winter, as was the norm) near the town, establishing good firing positions on the high ground in the vicinity. A period of standoff ensued during which Indian forces contemplated counterattacks—and Pakistani armed forces apparently at least began to ready nuclear launchers for possible use in turn. The crisis continued until President Bill Clinton forced Pakistani prime minister Nawaz Sharif to understand that his military's initial incursion into Indian-controlled Kashmir was the unacceptable precipitating action that caused the crisis—and that it needed to be unconditionally reversed. But in the meantime, the two nuclear-armed states walked up to the brink of direct conflict that some viewed as akin to their own Cuban missile crisis.[20] Attacks by Pakistan-based (and perhaps government-supported) terrorists against targets in India in 2001 and 2008 again raised the specter of war on the subcontinent. Had India responded with more than a small attack, and some in Pakistan worried about an all-out Indian invasion, there would likely have been pressures to ready nuclear weapons and perhaps even carry out a "demonstration strike" or other limited use to emphasize that Pakistan would not hesitate to use nuclear weapons to protect its national territory.[21]

Notionally at least, over the first sixty-five years of the nuclear age, it seems reasonable to conclude that the chances of nuclear weapons being used have "averaged" somewhere between 1 percent and 10 percent a decade. That number cannot be proved, of course, but is based on estimates ranging from Bundy's and Kennedy's over the Cuban missile crisis to a reading of what happened in Berlin to other cases. In the 1940s nuclear weapons were in fact used. In the 1950s there was at least modest risk of weapons being used during war or crisis in East Asia, or over Berlin. The 1960s were punctuated by the Cuban missile crisis. The 1970s witnessed numerous crises in the Middle East, culminating in the Carter Doctrine of 1980 declaring that the United States had a vital interest in the uninterrupted flow of Persian Gulf oil after the Soviet invasion of Afghanistan. The 1990s saw the locus of nuclear-related scares shift to South Asia, highlighted by the Kargil crisis of 1999.

Some would argue that the positive side of this real nuclear danger has been greater reluctance by the major powers to go to war among themselves even with conventional forces—a subject to which I return later in the book. Be that as it may, the fact is that we are becoming inured to a real risk of nuclear conflict as a reality of the modern world, and it is a reality that has hardly changed despite the end of the cold war.

In fact, the risk may be growing now. It is very significant that India and Pakistan, two countries that have fought four wars against each other in modern times, have nuclear weapons. Iran appears bent on acquiring the bomb, meaning that at least two countries (the other one being Israel) in the broader Middle East would then have such capabilities—at a time when Iran's current president has stated that Israel should be wiped off the face of the Earth, among other threatening comments. North Korea's nuclear arsenal may or may not create decisive pressures for other countries in Northeast Asia to acquire the bomb. Pakistan and North Korea have not only pursued their own weapons but have sought to share relevant technology with other countries—often for simple commercial motives. At various times in the recent past, potential recipient nations have included Iran, Libya, and Syria. Pakistan and especially North Korea add another risk to the equation: the possibility of state collapse in a country owning nuclear weapons, leaving the rest of the world with no clear ability to predict what would then happen to the country's nuclear arsenal.

These specific worries, and proliferation problems, also add up to a broader trend—toward what Assistant Secretary of State Kurt Campbell and former colleagues have pithily described as a possible "nuclear tipping point." The very notion that proliferation is not only undesirable but illegitimate—that only extremist states would even consider acquiring the bomb—is being challenged. The norm against building an arsenal may be weakening. So many countries now have nuclear weapons or seem on the path toward acquiring them that it is no longer unthinkable that "respectable" states would reassess their options as well, as a natural defensive response toward threatening developments within their neighborhoods. That this fear has existed before and been proven somewhat overblown does not eliminate the possibility that it could be realized in the future. Not only countries like Japan and perhaps South Korea, but also Taiwan, Turkey, and Saudi Arabia may feel the pressure.[22]

This danger of accelerating, self-reinforcing proliferation is a powerful motivator for the nuclear abolition movement. It is not the simple fact of more countries possessing the bomb that is necessarily so worrisome. It is, rather, a historical record that strongly suggests that countries with the bomb do in fact think about using it at times—or at least threatening to use it, creating dynamics that may not always prove easily controllable. The risks may also be greater for neighboring states with small arsenals than for the cold war superpowers. As Dick Betts writes, in response to the argument of Kenneth Waltz that nuclear proliferation can allegedly be good for international stability by inducing caution among states possessing the bomb,

> There are many technical and political counterarguments to Waltzian optimism about nuclear spread: poor countries' nuclear forces may be both small and vulnerable, creating the incentive for preventive attack; conflict dyads in many regions are between contiguous adversaries, precluding the tactical warning time of surprise attack on which U.S.-Soviet deterrence rested; animosities among contestants in some parts of the world (for example, Hindus vs. Muslims, Arabs vs. Israelis, Serbs vs. Albanians) are more intense and visceral than the tensions between Americans and Russians ever were, and the difference threatens cool calculation during crises.[23]

The words of McGeorge Bundy on the subject are a good way to conclude here. Bundy was in fact a relative optimist about how close the world came to nuclear war during the Cuban missile crisis (as well as at other perilous moments), having been not quite as worried as some that the world was on the nuclear precipice. Nonetheless, he wrote about nuclear war in 1962, "in this apocalyptic matter the risk can be very small indeed and still much too large for comfort."[24]

Accidents, Escalations, and Inadvertence

Calculated decisions to threaten or even use weapons of mass destruction in crises or in conflicts are not the only source of nuclear-related danger. Nuclear weapons and the organizations that control and operate them also can generate dangers of accidental, inadvertent, or unauthorized use. Indeed, such dynamics have already caused real-world scares. Although the major nuclear powers have taken some steps by now to mitigate such risks—including hotlines connecting their governments, permissive action links protecting warheads against unauthorized use, multiple-key arrangements ensuring that rogue individuals within governments cannot easily launch weapons without approval, and careful vetting of nuclear weapons personnel—the newer nuclear powers have not all done so systematically. And again, the simple fact that there has not yet been an accident leading to a nuclear detonation hardly proves that the world will forever be so fortunate.

In fact, there have already been closer calls than many remember today. The worst cases occurred decades ago, but the fact that they have begun to fade from memory hardly proves that they are no longer possible.

The opening paragraphs of Scott Sagan's classic book on nuclear safety are as good a way to motivate this concern as any other:

> On the night of October 25, 1962, an air force sentry was patrolling the perimeter of a military base near Duluth, Minnesota. It was the height of the Cuban missile crisis, and nuclear-armed bombers and interceptor aircraft, parked on air base runways and at commercial airports throughout the United States, were alert and ready for war. The sentry spotted someone climbing the base fence, shot at the figure, and sounded the sabotage alarm. At airfields throughout the region, alarms went off, and armed guards rushed into the cold night to prevent Soviet agents from sabotaging U.S. nuclear forces.
>
> At Volk Field in Wisconsin, however, the wrong alarm rang: the Klaxon signaling that nuclear war had begun went off. Pilots ran to their nuclear-armed interceptors and started the engines. These men had been told that there would be no practice alert drills during the tense crisis, and they fully believed that a nuclear war was starting as they headed down the runway. Fortunately, the base commander

contacted Duluth before the planes took off and discovered what had happened. An officer in the command post immediately drove his car onto the runway, flashing his lights and signaling the interceptors. The pilots saw him and stopped their aircraft. The suspected Soviet saboteur that caused the whole incident was, ironically, a bear.[25]

Other problems occurred during the 1962 missile crisis as well. A U.S. reconnaissance aircraft strayed over Soviet territory, and a routine intercontinental ballistic missile test launch was carried out despite its obvious potential to cause huge worries in Moscow.[26]

Simple accidents involving nuclear weapons, especially those carried by bombers in the days of continuous airborne alert of American nuclear weapons, occurred several times too. A B-52 with two bombs aboard collided with a refueling plane and crashed in 1959. Another B-52 broke apart in flight in 1961 and its two bombs fell to earth; that same year, yet another B-52 crashed on landing with two bombs in its weapons bay. A second collision of a B-52 with a refueling plane occurred in 1966, with four thermonuclear bombs falling to the ground. One was lost at sea for three months; three others fell on Spanish soil. The conventional explosives in two of the bombs promptly detonated, causing no nuclear reaction (given safety features on the weapons) but spreading radioactive debris. The third bomb was recovered largely intact. In 1968 a fire on a nuclear-armed B-52 flying over Greenland led the crew to eject. The bomber continued on in its flight, crashing and burning seven miles from Thule Air Base. The conventional high explosives (but not the nuclear materials) in all four bombs detonated.[27]

No country today maintains nuclear-armed aircraft on constant airborne alert. But things can change in a major crisis. Not only will weapons and their delivery platforms sometimes be raised to a higher state of readiness during crises. In addition, countries in such circumstances will feel pressure to give up the "negative control" of their arsenals, by which they reduce the risks of accidental or unauthorized launch in normal conditions through multiple layers of redundancy in their safety and security systems. They may move to a state of "positive control" of key nuclear forces, delegating some degree of launch authority to subordinate commanders to ensure the credibility of their deterrent even after a possible enemy first strike (which could incapacitate top leaders or disrupt lines of communication).

Other types of mishaps have occurred in the past as well, including problems with command, control, and warning. On the American side, in 1979 and again in 1980, false information about a Soviet nuclear attack occurred, one incident the result of operator error and another the consequence of a malfunctioning computer chip. Remedial measures were instituted thereafter. But again, there is no guarantee that such scenarios cannot recur—and there certainly is no guarantee that other countries will adopt similar safety and redundancy practices of their own.[28] The August 2007 incident in which Air Force personnel unknowingly and accidentally moved nuclear weapons within the United States, from Minot Air Force Base in North Dakota to Barksdale Air Force Base in Louisiana, underscores that such problems are not all in the past. While the mistake did not imperil anyone directly, it did, among other things, leave nuclear weapons unprotected for a certain time. The Air Force's capacity for losing track, even temporarily, of the whereabouts of nuclear weapons is quite disquieting—even if remedial steps have now been taken that probably make a similar occurrence in the foreseeable future much less likely.[29]

Command and control systems represent yet another degree of vulnerability, perhaps the greatest of all. As Bruce Blair convincingly argued in his landmark 1985 study of the U.S. nuclear command and control system, possible Soviet attacks against it were the most promising way to prevent an American retaliatory strike. In his words, "mutual command vulnerability creates strong incentives to initiate nuclear strikes before the opponent's threat to C-3-I [command, control, communications, and intelligence] could be carried out." In addition, such vulnerabilities mean that a very limited nuclear strike intended primarily to signal resolve in a crisis may lead very quickly to escalation because command systems are damaged (creating false information for one or both sides) or because the fear of losing the systems leads to deliberate rapid escalation (to cripple an opponent before he can escalate). To quote Blair again, "the pursuit of a bargaining advantage by means of limited attack is a purely intellectual construction that has little or no relevance to present circumstances." Those circumstances may have since changed for the superpowers, but they may still apply to smaller regional powers—whether those powers fully realize it or not.[30] Subsequent research about Soviet behavior during the cold war by David Hoffman and others indicates that Moscow was concerned about these problems too, creating a "dead hand" system to ensure missile launch even after national leaders might have been killed in a first strike.[31] Such virtual doomsday machines are not consistent with the notion of a stable nuclear balance.

So nuclear command and control could be vulnerable in any kind of nuclear exchange, even of a limited type, a fact that might surprise some leaders who had assumed their systems would be resilient and reliable. But the problem is even more serious. Especially for smaller powers, and for those nuclear rivals located close to each other, conventional military operations could threaten crucial nuclear infrastructure including command and control assets—even without the attacking country having any such intention. In other words, Country A might carry out strictly conventional operations against Country B that made the latter start to worry about the survivability of its nuclear deterrent—or at least about its ability to command and control that deterrent, which ultimately amounts to the same thing. In addition, Country B's warning systems could be weakened or compromised by the conventional fighting, making it unable to detect signs of future nuclear attack—or perhaps even producing false alarms that such an attack was under way. Not every country has separate command, control, and warning systems for conventional operations on the one hand and for nuclear operations on the other. Nor would an attacking country necessarily spare the crucial dual-purpose warning and command assets of an enemy just to preserve the workings of nuclear deterrence. Doing so would allow the enemy to operate more effectively at the conventional level and would therefore be a difficult form of restraint to expect out of a belligerent.

Barry Posen wrote a major study in 1991 about the possibility of inadvertent escalation as it might have affected the Soviet Union during the cold war; the problem could be even worse for countries like India and Pakistan today. As he put it then, for the case of a conflict in Europe, "in an air battle over Central Europe thousands of planes would have been in the air in circumstances that could easily have made Soviet leaders nervous: Soviet air defenses would probably have been degraded, NATO would almost surely have had nuclear-capable aircraft in the air, and the Soviets might well have felt that important strategic assets such as command, control, communications, and intelligence facilities were threatened." Posen goes on to underscore that such problems could be even worse for smaller powers sharing borders and thus having less strategic space to provide warning time and defense in depth.[32]

These kinds of structural realities of military forces, in addition to creating unintentional potential for escalation dynamics, also create the possibility of a successful and intentional surprise attack against enemy nuclear forces or their command and control networks. Given the effectiveness of well-executed surprise attacks in many historical cases, this type of scenario should not be dismissed lightly even regarding nuclear weapons and the nuclear age.[33]

It is also worth remembering that militaries sometimes develop quite elaborate war plans, such as the U.S. single integrated operational plan, or SIOP, that require fairly precise matching of weapons to targets. If other countries have acted similarly, their military planners might worry in the course of conventional or limited nuclear wars about losing their capability to carry out such integrated, coordinated attacks. That could lead to "use or lose" dynamics while there was still some hope of carrying out the original concept for nuclear strike, which could lead to escalation. In other words, internal war-fighting plans and procedures as well as organizational pressures can lead to incentives for rapid escalation.[34]

These kinds of worries did not end with the cold war. For example, in 1995 an unannounced launch of a Norwegian sounding rocket led to scares in Moscow about a possible nuclear attack. As a result the preliminary steps for activating Russia's emergency-response mechanisms for possible nuclear retaliation were initiated.[35]

Proliferation and Terrorism

The likelihood of terrorists getting their hands on a nuclear weapon, delivering it to a major city, and detonating it is a subject of great debate. But virtually no one questions that this horrible scenario is a real possibility in today's world.

Brian Michael Jenkins, himself a skeptic about the likelihood of a devastating terrorist nuclear strike and a critic of those who hype this scenario, nonetheless writes that "nuclear terrorism is a real threat."[36] The bomb designer, the late Ted Taylor, was convinced that if fissile materials fell into the wrong hands, terrorists or other extremists could well build a crude nuclear device. As renowned writer John McPhee wrote about Taylor, "he has satisfied himself to the point of certainty that a homemade nuclear bomb is not an impossibility, that such an undertaking need not even be particularly difficult, and that the people who could do it are countable in an expanding number that is already in the many tens of thousands."[37] And if al Qaeda or a similar group acquired a nuclear bomb, the chances seem very high that the terrorists would seek to use it—perhaps against Israel, perhaps against the United States. George Tenet, Bruce Riedel, and other analysts have carefully documented the degree to which al Qaeda has shown an acute interest in weapons of mass destruction including nuclear bombs over the years, and their findings are hard to dismiss.[38] Any terrorist group acquiring the bomb would have numerous ways to try to move it into a major Western city. None of these methods would be guaranteed to work. But many would have a real chance of success, given the difficulty of finding fissile materials or other telltale indicators of the presence of nuclear weapons using existing or foreseeable detection technologies.[39]

As far as is known, terrorists have not yet gotten their hands on significant quantities of weapons-grade fissile material. But there have been real scares nonetheless. When the Soviet Union broke apart, large quantities of bomb-usable material were poorly secured in a number of places for a period of time, including nearly 1,300 pounds of highly enriched uranium in Kazakhstan. Much more modest amounts of weapons-grade material were transferred illicitly. For example, a Russian named Yuri Smirnov stole modest amounts of highly enriched uranium from the Luch Scientific Production plant in 1992 and then tried to sell it.

The way Pakistan maintains its current nuclear arsenal of nearly 100 bombs—emphasizing secrecy over the physical security of weapons—gives rise to still other concerns. Pakistan has made serious efforts to create a dependable system, with some U.S. help and some success, as U.S. officials agree.[40] But this approach works only as long as insiders do not betray the system of safeguards, which relies on the complete dependability of a small number of people—a difficult precondition for any country to guarantee indefinitely.[41] Lest anyone assume that such problems, and security weaknesses, exist only in weak states or countries in transition, U.S. Navy SEALs "stole" several bombs' worth of plutonium in a 1998 drill at the Rocky Flats Nuclear Laboratory in Colorado.[42] That is, they gained access to sites where they were able to take custody of a substantial amount of fissile material.

Again, Brian Jenkins does well to keep our fears in check and to discourage any mass migration out of American cities or other types of responses based on panic and paranoia. For example, in response to the worry that terrorists may have gotten their hands on Russian suitcase bombs in the 1990s—a fear that seemed very real at the time—Jenkins points out that had they done so, they would likely have already used the bombs by now. And if they chose instead to squirrel the bombs away for a future use, the weapons might no longer be functional after so many years without expert maintenance.[43] But the fact that dangers are finite, and lower than some allege, does not mean that they are zero—or small enough for any semblance of comfort.

As more countries gain possession of nuclear weapons, and an even larger number of countries engages in nuclear commerce and power production, worries about the security of nuclear materials remain serious. Many materials are not well secured today, leading Harvard professor Graham Allison to call for a "Fort Knox" standard of security for all nuclear materials and weapons.[44] Even if such a standard were achievable, it would take time to achieve—and even a Fort Knox standard itself may not be foolproof. Indeed, such a standard is a useful goal but is probably not realistic given that many nuclear facilities are much smaller than Fort Knox and not in places where multiple robust layers of security can be established and maintained. The world should try to adopt Allison's idea, to be sure. He and other scholars like Harvard's Matt Bunn have usefully proposed strategies for securing the world's most dangerous nuclear materials within several years, with numerous suggestions about how to give incentives to other states to go along with such plans. Such ideas have led to progress in securing nuclear materials in Bulgaria, the Czech

Republic, Latvia, Libya, Poland, Romania, Serbia, Uzbekistan, and elsewhere. That said, as of recently, fissile materials remained unsecured in about 100 research reactors and other sensitive facilities in more than thirty countries.[45]

Of course, the distribution of global nuclear materials today is not static or fixed. It is evolving, and sometimes in dangerous ways. The clandestine network set up by Pakistani nuclear scientist A. Q. Kahn shows what is technically possible—that is, what can elude American and other global detection networks. Even if a rogue actor like Khan, protected as he was by irresponsible Pakistani governments of the time, is a rarity, the fact remains that nuclear-related technologies are difficult to monitor and fairly widespread around the world today. As such, a number of countries could choose to build illicit nuclear arsenals with a respectable chance of evading detection. Khan sold centrifuges and centrifuge designs, including for high-quality "P-2" machines, to several countries and transferred uranium gas (uranium hexafluoride, or UF6) as well. Iran, Libya, and North Korea were the key recipient countries (with some suspicions surrounding Syria too). This network of illicit nuclear commerce functioned for many years before human intelligence sources and good luck finally produced the leads that led to its dismantlement. By then, a great deal of lasting damage had been done, since countries like Iran have the technical and industrial capacity to produce their own equipment such as centrifuges now that they have been taught how to do so.[46] This is especially true in a world with uneven quality of export controls and enforcement mechanisms for preventing the unauthorized sales of dual-use technologies like advanced machine tools, aluminum alloys, and electronic triggering devices, which have been smuggled to would-be nuclear proliferators in the past.[47]

The nuclear power industry also presents major challenges. There is debate about just how much nuclear energy will increase in the coming decades but little doubt that it will spread at least somewhat.[48] Under the Nuclear Non-Proliferation Treaty (NPT), countries are entitled to develop not only nuclear reactors but a full nuclear fuel cycle including, if they wish, uranium enrichment and plutonium reprocessing technologies, provided that those technologies are put under formal safeguards monitored by the International Atomic Energy Agency (IAEA). This arrangement creates the potential for breakout, since countries can import centrifuges and the like, allegedly to make reactor fuel or dispose of waste, and later expel IAEA inspectors (as North Korea did in 2003) and produce bomb-usable fissile materials. The NPT can thereby, in a perverse way, worsen the proliferation problem by legitimating the spread of key nuclear technologies. This problem has been recognized and addressed to some extent. Tougher inspections are now required of nuclear sites under the "Additional Protocol" of the IAEA. Technologies related to the full fuel cycle are no longer allowed to be sold to Iran in particular (Teheran has not signed the Additional Protocol), and many key technology suppliers are wary in general about spreading enrichment or reprocessing technologies abroad. Still, even as some remedial steps are taken, other aspects of the challenge are intensifying, with Algeria, Belarus, Egypt, Indonesia, Jordan, Kazakhstan, Morocco, Nigeria, and Venezuela showing active interest in developing nuclear energy capabilities.[49] The problem will be greater still if plutonium reprocessing spreads in the future because of a global shortage of uranium fuel or a difficulty in disposing of waste.[50]

One could argue that the spread of nuclear technologies will make it harder, not easier, for the established nuclear powers to eliminate their arsenals, since they will have even more potentially nuclear-armed adversaries to deter. This is a reality that any serious nuclear disarmament proposal must wrestle with, as discussed later. But the ability of a would-be cheater to get away with such breakout behavior is perhaps greater in today's world than in the past, because the larger number of nuclear weapons states has partially eroded the stigma of developing the bomb. In addition, the punishments for most past proliferators have not been severe. When North Korea withdrew from the NPT in 2003, for example, the toughening of international sanctions was not particularly impressive.

A world of nine nuclear powers is already dangerous enough. A world with fifteen or twenty or twenty-five would likely be much more dangerous—both from the potential for nuclear weapons employment in a war between states and from the potential for terrorists to acquire nuclear materials or weapons. It is easy to imagine candidates for future proliferation if trends stay as they are—not only the "obvious suspects" of states like Iran, but also other Mideast countries in response, a number of East Asian states that could feel threatened by China or North Korea, countries in central Europe that might feel threatened by Russia, and perhaps other countries like Argentina and Brazil, or Venezuela and Colombia, that, although showing restraint to date, might engage in arms racing behavior in the future.[51]

Some causes of this trend toward more proliferation do derive from the existing arsenals of the world's nuclear states. Their arsenals complicate their ability to work together to pressure would-be proliferators into desisting from their nuclear ambitions. Perhaps that would be different if the nuclear states truly sought to eliminate their own arsenals. As Jonathan Schell compellingly argues, "today, for example, the United States, China, and Russia are disunited in their approach to Iranian violations of the NPT, with the United States taking a tough line and Russia and China taking a more permissive approach. But it is unimaginable that a Russia and China that were themselves planning to do without nuclear arms would permit an Iran or any other nation to develop them."[52] This is a question to which I return later. But first, the case *against* the elimination of the bomb must be acknowledged and discussed in some detail, for however much one might wish to ban nuclear weapons, doing so will be extremely difficult.

3 WHY ABOLITION IS IMPRACTICAL

THE ARGUMENTS FOR GETTING rid of nuclear weapons, rather than assuming that mankind can peacefully and safely coexist indefinitely with the bomb, are very strong. The problem is that abolition almost surely cannot be achieved—at least not in any absolute, permanent, unconditional sense. Proponents of abolition generally see nuclear weapons as the military and moral equivalent of slavery, as implied by the very lexicon they use to describe their goal. As a result, most believe that nuclear weapons must be eliminated comprehensively and permanently, without caveats or conditions (except in the event that one country violates the future nuclear weapons ban, at which point others would not be expected to continue honoring their obligations either). That goal seems excessive and unrealistic. Indeed, for reasons discussed in this chapter, it is also probably counterproductive. In other words, aiming too fast and too sweepingly for the eradication of nuclear weapons could actually encourage the very kinds of proliferant behavior that the nuclear disarmament vision is designed to counter and thus worsen rather than improve the planet's security.

Four main reasons underpin this conclusion. First and most directly, many proponents of abolition sweep aside challenges of verification as if they are just temporary impediments to designing a viable accord. I fear they are more fundamental, deriving as they do from the laws of physics together with the laws of human nature and state behavior. Second, the prospect that advanced biological weapons will someday be developed, with an extremist state perhaps even able to develop a vaccine to protect its own people against the superbug it has created, makes it hard to dismiss the value of nuclear deterrence. Third, those who believe that American and more generally Western conventional military superiority is the antidote to any and all such cheating, or the future development and use of weapons of mass destruction, are far too optimistic, and their arguments are often facile. Finally, for these and other reasons, pursuing nuclear disarmament quickly and carelessly can actually increase the incentives for key regional countries that currently depend on American security assurances to go nuclear themselves. By making them doubt the dependability of the U.S. commitment to their defense, the pursuit of nuclear disarmament could push them to look for alternatives.

My arguments against abolition as it is frequently advocated are not based on a deep-rooted sense that nuclear weapons are required for international stability. Nor are they based on theoretical arguments that small, safe, survivable nuclear deterrents in the hands of established international powers make for a safer world than would a nuclear disarmament system—a case that scholar Charles Glaser has articulated.[1] Since World War II ended, great-power stability has likely been determined at least as much by conventional military deterrence as by nuclear weapons, as John Mueller has argued.[2] The quality and nature of established governments also have evolved positively to some degree, perhaps out of awareness of what world war did to the planet in the relatively recent past, and if this trend is continued and expanded to include greater stability in Western relations with Russia as well as a resolution of the Taiwan problem, great-power peace would be even more strongly established on solid foundations.[3] But there are even more deep-rooted problems with most common visions of nuclear disarmament, even starker challenges to the viability of the basic idea.

In the next chapter I try to reconcile these problems and concerns with the very real arguments in favor of eliminating—or at least disabling and dismantling—nuclear arsenals as well as all bomb-ready fissile materials. It is there that I make the skeptic's case *for* nuclear disarmament. But this chapter first makes a skeptic's case *against* the view that nuclear abolition is viable on the terms often proposed.

The Challenges of Verification

Nuclear weapons, and the key materials inside of them, are hard to detect. This simple truth about the nature of verification challenges any global zero regime. This fact is not just a reflection of the current state of technology, or an indictment of current worthwhile institutions and efforts designed to impede proliferation such as the International Atomic Energy Agency (IAEA), the Proliferation Security Initiative, UN Security Council Resolution 1540 requiring states to improve nuclear safety measures including export controls, and the Nuclear Suppliers' Group export control regime. It is rather a basic reality deriving from the laws of physics—and more specifically the very limited radioactive signatures emitted by fissile materials—together with the possibility that even these weak signals might be reduced much further through shielding.

This reality is also of central importance in assessing the prospects for a nuclear disarmament treaty. Arms control critics and skeptics alike have long argued that verification must be able to detect militarily significant violations of any accord by one party in time for other parties to take reciprocating actions. In the context of superpower arms control, when both sides had thousands of survivable second-strike warheads that could not be eliminated by the other side under any plausible circumstances, the margin for error according to this definition was greater. Cheating would have been, and was, a very bad thing for what it signified about the other side's trustworthiness. It also caused concerns about the other side's intentions and commitment to pursue peace. But cheating did not create fundamental military vulnerabilities; for example, the United States was never at serious risk of being disarmed by a Soviet first strike that consisted of more missiles and warheads than a treaty allowed.

With a nuclear disarmament regime, the situation could be very different. If one side truly disarmed, even a small number of warheads in the hands of another country could have enormous military implications. The significance of these implications would depend in part on the state of air and missile defenses as well as homeland security capabilities of other countries; to have a truly potent threat, the aggressor would likely need to be able to deliver its weapons against others with some degree of confidence. (I return to the subject of what such defenses should look like in any world free of nuclear weapons in chapter 4.) But if the country in question did have some means of credibly threatening successful delivery, the situation would be stark. Being able to destroy even a small number of cities in other places would give the country a potentially decisive war-fighting advantage.

To be sure, destruction or threatened destruction of cities has not historically ended most wars, as the conventional bombing experiences of World War II underscore. Debate continues about the role of nuclear weapons in forcing Japan's surrender in 1945, with some historians arguing that the cumulative effects of many attacks on Japanese cities (most with conventional bombs) together with the specter of possible Soviet intervention played a greater role.[4] Nor have nuclear weapons states been consistently able to translate their weapons capabilities into military victories against lesser powers.[5] But these arguments are not conclusive. Historical counterexamples about the potential potency of even conventional airpower exist. Notable was Serbia's capitulation when NATO's rather humane but still debilitating air campaign intensified against Belgrade in 1999, even if other factors also played a role.[6] In any case, the future behavior of countries when faced with nuclear threats and no means of dependable defense or prompt reprisal cannot be confidently forecast. In principle, an aggressor might be able to coerce very quickly the surrender of another state, before that country could arm or rearm itself with a nuclear deterrent as a means of defense. The attacker might even destroy another country's key war-fighting and nuclear industries as well as its seat of government—preventing any realistic chance for rearmament and retaliation, nuclear or otherwise, by the attacked state.

Given the realities of basic physics, it is difficult to see how any nuclear disarmament regime could truly ensure that illicit fissile materials or actual bombs did not exist and were not being built. Clever ideas may help in the future, to be sure. But the challenge is daunting. How can one find fissile materials? The most logical approach is to look for the "signatures" or emissions, spontaneous or induced, of these elements that are distinctive and visible. However, the particles given off by plutonium or uranium through natural radioactive decay are few and far between—and fairly easily shielded by materials like lead. Most of the recent innovations in detection technology work only when they are in very close proximity to the nuclear materials, and that will remain true with the next generation of detectors.[7] They can be used at entry points to a country, where containers may be imported; at monitored production and storage facilities (or nuclear power plants), to detect any hidden nuclear materials that are being moved in or out; and at other sensitive locations worthy of extra layers of protection. But they are severely constrained in other settings.

Passive detectors that look for the signatures emitted naturally by radioactive materials may find plutonium or uranium at distances of several meters. Active detectors that fire one type of radiation or another at a suspicious site and look for telltale responses indicating the presence of fissile materials can work at somewhat greater distances. They are not, however, usable to search for materials at a distance of a kilometer or even hundreds of meters. Even if detection improves in coming decades through technologies such as muon radiography, finding nuclear facilities deep within a country's territory, where facilities could be tens of kilometers away from even low-altitude orbiting satellites, will remain very difficult.[8]

One can of course look for the facilities that produce fissile materials. Currently, uranium enrichment generally requires either large diffusion plants, which are conspicuous in their size and power requirements, or centrifuge facilities, which require large numbers of identical well-machined rotors. Plutonium production requires nuclear reactors that give off large heat signatures.

However, finding even these facilities is not guaranteed. For example, Iran's nuclear enrichment plant at Natanz was revealed by dissident groups—human intelligence, in 2002—not by satellite or other remote means.[9] The kind of electromagnetic isotope separation ("calutron") technology used by Saddam's Iraq in the 1980s, inefficient and small-scale as it is, is nonetheless capable of enriching uranium and hard to detect as well.[10] Future technologies such as laser isotope enrichment facilities may be even harder to locate from a distance.

Because the technical means of locating fissile materials are of such limited capability—and will remain limited—much recent effort in arms control has focused on strengthening human intelligence networks so that dissidents, whistleblowers, and others with direct knowledge of a country's program to develop nuclear weapons capability feel emboldened, and protected enough, to speak out. These ideas about so-called societal verification are worthwhile and can help with any nuclear disarmament effort too. But they provide a certain statistical probability of detection rather than a dependable way of finding an illicit program in the limited amount of time that might be available during a breakout scenario by a cheating country with aggressive designs. A country breaking out of a nuclear disarmament accord in the space of just a few years at most might be able to conceal key sites long enough to achieve its core purposes. To be sure, not everything of nuclear significance is small and easily concealable. Nuclear reactors are harder to hide. Reprocessing facilities that extract bomb-usable plutonium from spent fuel can also sometimes be found through their krypton-85 signatures that show up in air samples. But uranium enrichment capabilities are, alas, on balance easier to hide.

As nuclear energy technology spreads further around the globe, the challenge grows even more difficult. Numerous reactors already exist in the United States and Canada, western and central Europe, Japan and South Korea, Russia, China, and Taiwan, India and Pakistan, Argentina and Brazil, Mexico, and South Africa. Belarus, Indonesia, and Iran are building or planning to build nuclear reactors. Bahrain, Bangladesh, Egypt, Jordan, Kazakhstan, Kuwait, Oman, Qatar, Saudi Arabia, the United Arab Emirates, Thailand, and Vietnam have taken concrete steps to explore options about or solicit providers of nuclear reactors. Algeria, Azerbaijan, Ghana, Libya, Morocco, Nigeria, the Philippines, Tunisia, Venezuela, and Yemen are also believed to be exploring nuclear energy options. Australia, Kazakhstan, Mongolia, Namibia, Niger, and Uzbekistan do not have nuclear power reactors but do possess major natural uranium resources.[11]

Under any nuclear disarmament accord, all major nuclear facilities worldwide would have to be declared and monitored—playing to the strengths of detection technologies, which are indeed getting better at short range. And under some recent proposals, such as the idea of then–IAEA director Mohamed El Baradei, new enrichment facilities would be allowed only as part of multinational consortia—perhaps making breakout strategies more difficult to implement.[12] Similar restrictions would need to be employed for any plutonium reprocessing plants—though pursuit of nuclear disarmament would certainly be much more practical if they could be eliminated altogether, since the plutonium coming out of such plants is virtually bomb-ready.[13] But even with such restrictions, countries could still keep their declared enrichment facilities on the up and up, yet build additional clandestine facilities using the expertise they had gained from their legal activities. Most plausible proposals for limiting the diffusion of enrichment technologies, for example, would still allow a greater number of countries to own such facilities than is the case today, along with the kinds of machining plants needed to build centrifuges and similar technology. President George W. Bush's proposal for sharing future nuclear energy technology would not have allowed additional countries to enrich, but that idea seems unlikely to gain favor from most nations; other proposals would allow technologies to spread.[14]

A study group known as the International Panel on Fissile Materials put it well, in summarizing the challenges posed by the nuclear energy industry:

> If countries are allowed to separate plutonium from spent power-reactor fuel—as it is done today in France, India, Japan, Russia, and the United Kingdom—they could use this plutonium to make nuclear weapons within weeks. Countries with large national enrichment plants could similarly quickly begin to make large quantities of HEU [highly enriched uranium] for weapons. . . . The breakout times would be longer in a world without reprocessing and where states lacked national enrichment plants. But a state with nuclear reactors still could build a "quick and dirty" reprocessing plant and recover plutonium from spent power reactor fuel within six months to a year.[15]

In addition to the difficulties of detecting new sources of illicit nuclear materials, any nuclear disarmament regime would face nontrivial tasks in verifying the dismantlement of existing warheads and the transformation or irretrievable elimination of existing stocks of fissile materials. A good deal of excellent work has already gone into understanding this task, as reflected, for example, in George Perkovich and James Acton's recent publications. But this work also underscores the degree of the challenge. For example, in discussing existing stockpiles, particularly of the superpowers, Perkovich and Acton write that "substantial uncertainties in fissile material inventories are unavoidable. Even with blameless intentions and honest accounting, such uncertainties would be on the order of a few percent of production." These uncertainties arise because the existing weapons states have destroyed material through testing, not always accurately measured the amount of fissile material lost in waste streams, and otherwise failed to maintain rigorous monitoring and accounting. As a result, nuclear powers today do not know themselves exactly how much usable fissile material they possess.[16] Russia and the United States in particular have had enough problems with their bookkeeping efforts over the years that it may not be possible to account accurately for about 1 percent of the world's current fissile materials—enough for 1,000 bombs.

In addition to the nuclear power and research reactors around the globe, today a dozen states have uranium enrichment plants. Several use HEU or relatively highly enriched uranium to power naval vessels. Ten have plutonium reprocessing plants. Any meaningful verification regime would have to track these materials too. The challenge here is daunting.[17]

The Threat from Biological Arms

Nuclear abolitionists often argue that not all weapons of mass destruction are created equal. And even though the term seems to imply otherwise, they are surely right. Chemical weapons are cruel and potent killers. But they are relatively hard to deliver in most places (although the use of sarin or a comparable high-quality and lethal agent in the air circulation systems of large buildings and other public facilities is a nontrivial threat, and of course completely unsuspecting and undefended civilian populations can suffer greatly as Iraq's Saddam Hussein showed with his use of chemical weapons in the brutal al-Anfal campaign against the Kurds in 1988).

While the notion of biological weapons conjures up horrible images of incurable and fatal diseases that create slow, painful death, their actual use to date has been so restricted that the perceived potency of the threat has diminished in the eyes of many. In addition, given their typically slow incubation times, and indiscriminate effects, they often have been seen, rightly, as instruments of terror rather than of purposeful state violence. This is not to deny that existing agents could be very lethal, only that they would have to be disseminated extremely effectively and in a manner not yet witnessed. That highly contagious agents have not yet been combined with deadly ones further constrains the magnitude of the existing threat. That does not mean the world can safely forget about biological weapons, but it arguably does refute the notion that nuclear weapons would be an appropriate deterrent to their use against the United States or its friends and allies.

The United States has at times recognized this reality. It has publicly committed not to use nuclear weapons against nonnuclear states (unless the latter are allied with nuclear powers in wartime operations). It did that, for example, during the 1995 review conference of the Nuclear Non-Proliferation Treaty (NPT). Yet the policy has not been consistent. Even while making such commitments at various points in the nuclear era, the United States has also wanted to retain nuclear weapons as an explicit deterrent against other, nonnuclear forms of weapons of mass destruction as a matter of targeting policy and nuclear weapons doctrine.[18] The Obama administration's Nuclear Posture Review reduces the contradiction but does not eliminate it, because nuclear weapons could in theory be used against the (nonnuclear) capabilities of countries violating their NPT obligations or, someday, against countries that had developed more advanced biological pathogens than are currently available.

The American pledge not to use nuclear weapons against non-nuclear states is inconsistent when it is combined with an American willingness to consider using nuclear weapons in response to a biological (or chemical) attack. As a normal matter of policy, the United States should *not* plan on any nuclear response to any attacks by lesser types of weapons of mass destruction, especially the types of attacks that might be anticipated today or that have been witnessed in the recent past (for example, the chemical attacks during the Iran-Iraq war of the 1980s).[19]

But things could change in the future. Biological weapons could become much more potent or be dispersed far more efficiently than has been the case. Biological knowledge certainly is advancing fast. To take one metric, the number of genetic sequences on file, a measure of knowledge of genetic codes (short or long) for various organisms, grew from well under 5 million in the early 1990s to 80 million by 2006.[20] The number of countries involved in biological research is growing rapidly too. For Americans, who long led the way in biology, it is sobering and important to remember that today, at least half of all important biological research is being done abroad. For a movement focused on the future, many nuclear abolitionists have not squarely faced the challenge of biological weapons as they could evolve and improve in coming decades.

One thoughtful and well-argued study in the 1990s asserted that nuclear weapons should never be used against biological (or chemical) threats or in retaliation for such attacks. However, that argument was more persuasive regarding the technologies of the day than for a hypothetical situation in the future. In considering the possibility of an extremely destructive biological agent that killed as many as nuclear weapons might, the authors wrote that "it would be technically and operationally difficult to achieve such high numbers of casualties with biological weapons, and no nation is known to possess weapons so effective."[21] True enough for the weapons of the day—and true enough for the agenda of that book, which was to promote deep cuts and de-alerting of nuclear forces. But what about twenty-five or fifty years from now, when the issue is the complete and permanent abolition of nuclear weapons?

One can naturally hope that better monitoring and verification concepts will be developed for biological and chemical weapons— just as they must clearly be improved in the nuclear realm if abolition is ever to be feasible.[22] But these will be very hard to devise and probably rather imperfect in their ability to provide timely warning. Various forms of direct and indirect monitoring can be tried—the latter including looking for mismatches between the numbers of trained scientists in a given country and the professional positions available to them there, or a mismatch between the numbers of relevant scientists and associated publications.[23] Big disparities could suggest hidden weapons programs. One can also build up disease surveillance systems and create rapid-response biological weapons investigation teams to look into any suspected development of illicit pathogens or any outbreak of associated disease.[24] But a good deal of luck would likely still be needed to discover most biological weapons programs.

Microbiological research often takes place in small facilities that are hard if not impossible to identify through remote sensing.[25] Various inspection regimes, export control regimes, and enhanced biological safety regimes have been proposed to reduce the risks of pathogens being developed by irresponsible actors. But the rigor of on-site inspections has to be balanced with companies' legitimate interests in protecting industrial secrets if and when they develop a new commercial product, adding to the challenge. And no inspection regime can confidently thwart the actions of a sophisticated state actor bent on developing advanced pathogens secretly; the technologies are becoming too ubiquitous, and the possibility of hiding illicit activities is too great.[26]

Countries bent on cheating are likely to succeed in hiding their associated facilities, at least for a time.

For such reasons, it is eminently possible that a future aggressor state could secretly develop an advanced "bug"—perhaps an influenza-born derivative of smallpox resilient against currently available treatments, for example. This bug could combine the contagious qualities of the flu with the lethality of very severe diseases.[27] It is such a prospect that leads John Steinbruner to note that "one can imagine killing more people with an advanced pathogen than with the current nuclear weapons arsenals."[28]

The state developing this bug might simultaneously develop a vaccine or new antibiotic to protect its own people against the new disease. That could be difficult, of course, in light of the technical challenges; for example, new classes of antibiotics are proving very difficult to develop.[29] Even if successfully developed, such a treatment might not be completely effective and might work less well over time—for example, the effectiveness of a vaccine designed to defeat a virus could atrophy if the original virus mutated. But a sufficiently extremist regime might be willing to throw the dice—especially since its real goal may be to intimidate other countries into backing down *before* war. It might try to coerce a country it was interested in conquering or taking land from. Or the target of any threats could be the broader international community, to deter foreign actors from coming to the rescue of the state being threatened or attacked directly (analogous to the specter of chemical and biological warfare Saddam used to try to deter the U.S.-led coalition from coming to Kuwait's aid in 1990–91). If the United States faced the prospect of millions of its own citizens becoming sick as it considered a response to a brutal aggression, and its only recourse was conventional retaliation, its range of options could be very limited. Indeed, the very troops called on to carry out the retaliation might become vulnerable to the disease, jeopardizing their physical capacity to execute the conventional operation. Perhaps they could be protected on the battlefield, once suited up, but they could be vulnerable before deployment (along with the rest of the American population). A potential adversary, sensing these possibilities, might find the concept of such an advanced pathogen very appealing.

Would there really be a clear and definitive moral argument against the use of a nuclear weapon in retaliation for a biological weapons attack that killed hundreds of thousands—or even millions—of innocent Americans? Locating the origin of an attack or of a biological pathogen that had not yet been used but had been somehow sampled could be challenging. But detection might well prove possible under numerous scenarios like the one sketched above.[30] If huge numbers of American civilians including the young, old, infirm, and sickly had been targeted, the case for restraint would be hard to make. At least, it would be no stronger than the case for absorbing a nuclear weapons strike and choosing not to retaliate.

What if the United States thought a biological attack by an aggressor imminent? Or what if it had already suffered one such attack, and others, against additional parts of the country, seemed possible. Would there really be no potential value, and no moral justifiability, in a nuclear threat against the belligerent state warning that any future use of biological attacks against the American people or their allies might produce a nuclear response?[31]

In his classic book on just and unjust war, Michael Walzer asserts that "nuclear war is and will remain morally unacceptable, and there is no case for its rehabilitation." He also argues that "nuclear weapons explode the theory of just war. They are the first of mankind's technological innovations that are simply not encompassable within the familiar moral world." This would seem to argue (since biological weapons of certain types predated nuclear technologies) that in fact nuclear threats could never be justifiable against a biological attack. However, the logic of Walzer's overall case against nuclear weapons is based explicitly on their indiscriminate and extreme effects—characteristics that advanced biological pathogens, which did not truly exist when he wrote these words, would share. To be sure, the entire concept of nuclear deterrence is one of questionable morality—and Walzer is right to demand that an alternative be sought as quickly as possible. That said, it is hard to argue that nuclear deterrence of an adversary's possible use of nuclear weapons is any less moral or justifiable than nuclear deterrence of an adversary's possible dissemination of an advanced pathogen that could kill millions.[32]

Indeed, a nuclear response to such a biological attack might possibly be done in a *more* humane way than the biological attack— if that was desired in a given situation. Nuclear responses might target military bases and command headquarters, for example, avoiding populated areas except where those leaders most directly responsible for the initial aggression were being targeted. To be sure, civilians would also be killed in such a nuclear attack; this reality cannot be denied. But in proportionate terms, a nuclear retaliatory blow could well cause fewer casualties among innocent civilian populations than would a biological pathogen. Some favor developing smaller and more discriminate nuclear weapons for such purposes. I do not, for reasons discussed later. But even today's weapons could be used in relatively discriminating ways—targeting remote yet important military bases selectively, for example, and doing so with existing lower-yield weapons fused to create airbursts rather than groundbursts, so radioactive contamination of downwind areas would be minimized.[33]

Bear in mind what is possible, at least theoretically, with engineered pathogens. As John Steinbruner notes, in discussing the contagiousness of certain flu-borne ailments, "one strain infected an estimated 80 percent of the world's population in a six-month period. Normally the incidence of disease among those infected is relatively low, as is the mortality rate of those who contract the disease. However, aviary strains of the virus have killed virtually all of the birds infected, which suggests the possibility of highly lethal human strains as well."[34]

No nuclear disarmament regime should inadvertently encourage the proliferation of biological weapons; any such regime needs to follow the Hippocratic oath of first doing no harm. It is thus important not to risk sending a message that a state producing a superbug, as well as a vaccine to protect its own people from that bug, could find itself with a war-winning strategy and escape many types of retaliation in the process. The international community need not be explicit about exactly if or when it would respond in this way. By the same token, however, the international community should not give sanctuary to such a proliferator. A nuclear disarmament regime must be designed to anticipate such superbug scenarios and have mechanisms for responding to them. It should deter the development and possible use of advanced biological agents in the first place, while reassuring nonnuclear allies that they need not develop their own nuclear arsenals to address such a contingency.

The Limitations of Conventional Military Superiority

Proponents of abolition often make the case that whatever the potential need for nuclear weapons may have been before, the need is far less now. Perhaps a war-fatigued nation had the right to use nuclear weapons against Japan in 1945 rather than risk a lengthy and bloody invasion of the Japanese home islands that could have killed a million or given the Soviet Union a foothold there. Perhaps there was little choice other than to rely on a measure of nuclear deterrence against the Soviet Union and its Warsaw Pact allies as they built up huge conventional military forces next to key U.S. allies in Europe during the cold war—and as the Western world sought to strengthen itself economically rather than consume huge amounts of collective GDP maintaining large traditional armies, navies, and air forces. But surely today, with the United States accounting for almost half of global defense spending and its allies another 30 to 35 percent, with American conventional military dominance so vividly on display in the invasions of Afghanistan and then Iraq (to say nothing of the effectiveness of NATO airpower in Kosovo in 1999), no serious case can be made that nuclear deterrence would be a more economical way to preserve Western security.[35] The United States and its allies could always deal with any aggressor—even one using chemical weapons, for example, and even one attacking a neighbor far from the United States or any of its major military bases—through strictly conventional means. So goes the argument, according to some.

Operation Desert Storm in 1991 provides a recent and relevant case on the potential role of nuclear weapons in the current international system. Some attributed Saddam's restraint in employing chemical or even biological weapons against the U.S.-led coalition to fear of a nuclear response by Washington. Iraq's foreign minister at the time, Tariq Aziz, and the head of military intelligence, General Wafic Al Sammarai, are both on record stating that they believed American nuclear retaliation was likely against any Iraqi use of chemical weapons.[36] Scott Sagan and others have argued, however, that the fear of a conventional operation to overthrow the Iraqi regime might have affected Saddam's calculations even more than worry about a possible American nuclear strike.[37]

Some scholars note, too, that nuclear weapons are not as cheap as often claimed. Steve Schwartz calculated that U.S. expenditures on nuclear systems from 1940 through 1996 approached $6 trillion in 1996 dollars—meaning closer to $9 trillion in 2010 dollars.[38] If one extends the calculation to include costs since 1996, the figure approaches $10 trillion. Schwartz and Deepti Choubey have recently estimated the ongoing nuclear-related costs of the United States at more than $50 billion a year. That estimate can be challenged. Schwartz and Choubey count all the costs of the U.S. bomber force and missile defense capabilities in their tally (even though these currently are intended largely for nonnuclear missions). They also count American nuclear safety and security programs focused on other countries' nuclear weapons arsenals in their accounting of U.S. nuclear weapons costs.[39] More cautious calculations by organizations such as the Congressional Budget Office suggest annual totals at least half as great, for both the cold war totals and the annual averages—still huge money.[40] If nuclear weapons are not cheap, and if the United States and its allies hold overwhelming conventional military dominance, the case for keeping nuclear weapons and nuclear deterrence would seem especially hard to sustain.

However, it is difficult to argue in the twenty-first century that nuclear deterrence will never again be relevant to deterring conventional war. I do not advocate, as a matter of official national military doctrine, preserving nuclear options for responding to conventional aggression. But the possible need cannot be categorically dismissed. Put it differently: if, in a future decade or century, a hostile country or group of countries builds threatening nonnuclear forces and plans on using them, in a manner evocative of World War II both in the destructiveness of the attacks and the ambitions of the aggressors, why should other countries not have the option of developing nuclear weapons in response? Even more to the point, it is simply not plausible that a treaty written anytime soon would make status-quo powers feel prohibited from building nuclear arms in such a threatening situation. This generation cannot be so clairvoyant, or so restrictive, about the future options and actions of its progeny.

Whatever the verdict about whether the threat of nuclear or conventional weapons weighed more in Saddam's decisionmaking, for example, there is little reason to assume that the architecture of the international system today is permanent or that the relative rankings of power among the world's major nations are likely to endure. Perhaps the challenges of the world in the 1940s and then in the cold war were unusual and are unlikely to recur. But the notion that a period of "benign hegemony," as some call the recent historical period of American-led great-power stability, is now a fixture of the international system is almost surely too optimistic.

Several reasons suggest that things will change. First, China is clearly bent on catching up—at least in some areas—with the United States and with key American allies such as Japan. This is particularly true of conventional military forces, it would appear. In addition, China is modernizing its nuclear weapons program, and even if the main purpose is to preserve a survivable second-strike force as officials and scholars generally claim, the result of this buildup will be a more advanced arsenal.[41] Second, the United States may not be able to sustain its large defense budgets indefinitely; the very dominance that so reassures nuclear abolitionists is seen as a provocative and wasteful level of spending by many. With U.S. budget deficits so high, the argument that a strong national defense requires a strong economy may lead to downward pressure on U.S. defense spending in future years.

Moreover, defense spending levels do not determine combat outcomes. Spending more on defense gives the United States certain real advantages in war fighting and deterrence, but it hardly ensures victory in every war or stability through every period of international crisis. Even today the United States could lose wars; certainly, Americans could determine as a nation that the cost of victory is too high for certain conflicts that, although winnable in theory, would be very difficult for the United States and its close allies to handle in practice.

Indeed, after overwhelming initial victories in Iraq and Afghanistan, the United States has struggled mightily in both places against determined insurgent forces. Each of those forces probably had an effective budget of less than $1 billion a year, or perhaps 500 to 1,000 times less than that of the United States. Each of those opposition movements was far smaller even in manpower than the U.S. coalition forces aligned against it. Yet each almost won, and, as of this writing, the Afghanistan opposition may yet prevail. What would happen, one wonders, in a war against a nation state of 100 million or 200 million people, able to employ a combination of conventional military forces, irregular methods, and perhaps weapons of mass destruction against nearby enemies and any foreign invading and occupying forces? Is it really so obvious that the United States and like-minded allies would be able, resoundingly and quickly, to defeat such a foe? The challenge could be greatest if the aggressor were successful in invading and occupying a neighbor; reversing that aggression could prove quite difficult, since at that point the aggressor might be able to profit from irregular methods to complicate the counterinvasion.

This is a specific illustration of a larger point: predicting outcomes in war is extremely hard. As Australian historian Geoffrey Blainey notes, for example, "when nations prepare to fight one another, they have contradictory expectations of the likely duration and outcome of the war. . . . it is doubtful whether any war since 1700 was begun with the belief, by *both* sides, that it would be a long war. . . . No wars are unintended or 'accidental.' What is often unintended is the length and bloodiness of the war. Defeat too is unintended."[42]

There is a reason so many people have been so unsuccessful in predicting the course of armed conflict: war depends greatly on hard-to-quantify variables, such as the quality of leadership, the effectiveness of any surprise, and the performance of new weapons systems or military operational concepts not previously tested in battle (and hence not well understood in advance of combat). Success on the battlefield is certainly not just about money or respective levels of defense investment and technology.

According to historical data, even if one country or alliance is clearly stronger than another, as indicated by various military metrics such as overall manpower or combat equipment inventories, high-confidence predictions about which side will win a given war are very hard to make. Johns Hopkins professor Joshua Epstein made this point clearly by analyzing evidence from the U.S. Army Concepts Analysis Agency published in the 1980s. The agency had gathered data on many past wars, which it used to compute overall scores on the capabilities of attackers and defenders. For countries with roughly comparable military capabilities, with neither side having more than a 50 percent edge against the other in military inputs, the data showed the attacker winning 142 of 230 battles, or 58 percent of the total.[43] There was no tendency toward stalemate (only 7 percent of all cases). Nor did the defender (who prevailed in just 35 percent of all cases) have a major inherent advantage.[44] Moreover, even though the attacking country usually won, victory was far from assured. The attacking side won only 63 percent of the time when having an estimated advantage between 50 percent and 200 percent over its opponent, and only 74 percent of the time when having an even greater edge.[45] So even when military balances seem to clearly favor one side, outcomes are hard to forecast.[46]

The tyranny of distance introduces an added challenge in predicting the outcomes of war. Potential enemies need not give fair notice of intention to attack U.S. allies, of course. They can try to act fast, before American reinforcements can arrive and while local military balances still favor them, and hope to pull off a fait accompli that the U.S. government and American public will decide not to challenge given the likely pain and cost of doing so. The difficulty, and slow pace, of deploying large numbers of military forces halfway around the world must be remembered in this context. Despite the hopes of military revolutionaries and proponents of a transformation in the ways of war, modern military forces remain large and heavy—and thus difficult to move.

The fact that military transportation is difficult should be obvious from the broad numbers—preparing for a major war overseas may not involve building skyscrapers or schools or factories, but it can require relocating most other elements of the equivalent of a midsize city like Washington, D.C. (population 550,000). In Operation Desert Storm, the United States moved not only half a million people and more than 100,000 vehicles, but a total of about 10 million tons of supplies (more than 6 million of which were petroleum products). Moving a force of 200,000 to 500,000

U.S. troops to a distant battlefield, despite huge efforts at improving transport and logistics capabilities over the years, still takes several months. Bottlenecks often develop at ports and airfields. Many airfields have limited space for loading and unloading aircraft, for example, and perhaps limited refueling capacity as well, severely constraining throughput. Even at reasonably large, modern airfields, deploying about 1,000 tons of equipment and supplies a day is generally the limit.[47] Absent at least three to four functioning ports and airfields in the theater of destination, therefore, maximum deployment rates would not be attainable. In fact, actual deployment rates are often less than half of what is mathematically feasible in the abstract. That means a few weeks would be needed for the United States to deploy a division-sized force and at least a few months to deploy a large force to most parts of the world.[48]

Some argue, as noted above, that the speed of deployment will improve with time. They envision an era of rapid, long-range, low-mass military responsiveness in which next-generation technologies will obviate the need for large deployments of huge armies. Perhaps. But if there is a single striking area of technology in which progress has not been revolutionary in recent decades, it is in the basics of how vehicles are powered—and fueled—on the battlefield. Visionaries about future war have talked about fast jets bouncing along the troposphere and covering intercontinental distances in two hours, or weapons in space being de-orbited to strike rapidly and precisely at targets on the ground, or ground armies quintupling their speeds while reducing fivefold or tenfold the number of forces they need to accomplish a given mission. But a careful examination shows fairly definitively that such visions are not within reach in the foreseeable future. The following language used in the well-regarded 1997 National Defense Panel report is thus too sweeping to be accurate: "The rapid rate of new and improved technologies—a new cycle about every eighteen months—is a defining characteristic of this era of change."[49]

Indeed, for many areas of engine and propulsion technology, one can debate whether a new cycle of technology comes even every eighteen years, if one focuses on the fundamentals of fuel consumption and speed.

Of course, modern jet fighters are faster than before, their engines burn at hotter temperatures, and they can go further and faster on supercruise. Catamaran-hull ships can attain speeds of fifty knots or more. Per pound of vehicle mass, modern internal combustion engines are more efficient than their predecessors. And next-generation combat vehicles are intended to require much less fuel than Abrams tanks. But, in fact, transport planes and ships as well as main warships, aircraft carriers and submarines, ballistic missiles and space launch vehicles, and battlefield trucks continue to plow along at roughly the same speeds, without radically reduced fuel requirements, relative to their predecessors of two or three or even four decades ago. Progress is measured in improvements of 10 and 25 percent from one generation of vehicle to another, not a doubling of capability and speed every eighteen to twenty-four months as with computers.[50] If next-generation main combat vehicles require less fuel than today's big tanks and fighting vehicles, it will likely be largely because they will be smaller and lighter—and, inevitably, more vulnerable to direct fire, given the modest incremental rates of progress in armor.[51] The internal combustion engine of today is better than that of earlier decades, but not radically so. Predictions like that offered by a knowledgeable observer in 1997 that the speeds of battlefield maneuver for major ground forces might increase from 40 kilometers an hour in Operation Desert Storm to 200 kilometers an hour by 2010 can now be seen as incorrect (with speeds in 2010 actually much closer to 40 than 200 kilometers an hour).[52]

When long-distance deployments take time to prepare, and when casualties are likely to be large, marshaling American political will to respond to aggression can be difficult. The prospect of high casualties remains a deterrent to American involvement in conflicts that are seen as wars of choice rather than wars of necessity.[53] And war often entails the prospect of significant losses. Even when ultimate outcomes in wars can be fairly confidently predicted, costs and casualties often cannot. For example, estimates of likely American losses before Operation Desert Storm ranged into the tens of thousands—including from the Pentagon's own models. Actual fatalities from all causes were less than 500. By contrast, estimates of U.S. losses in the invasion of Iraq were often in the range of hundreds—but now, nearly a decade later, the United States has lost some 5,000 there. Few predicted substantial losses in Afghanistan—where the number of American dead now number more than 1,000—especially after the initial overthrow of the Taliban in 2001 went so quickly and relatively easily.

The notion that a U.S.-led posse of democratic states can be expected to keep the international peace against any and all acts of aggression, or even classic interstate aggression, with conventional forces alone is highly optimistic. It is not a sound assumption on which to base a future world without nuclear weapons.

One can debate how much more deterrence nuclear weapons provide than conventional forces do. And reliance on nuclear weapons has ethical and moral downsides. But the argument that overwhelming U.S. conventional superiority has somehow made nuclear deterrence obsolete—by giving the United States straightforward options to overthrow an aggressor regime with conventional forces rather than respond to a biological attack or acts of genocide or other atrocities with nuclear weapons—is ahistorical and probably incorrect. I would not envision using American or other nuclear weapons against acts of conventional aggression in most scenarios. But exceptions could arise, for example a case involving genocide by one country against another deep in the heart of Eurasia—far from the kinds of bases that would allow traditional American and other international military forces to move in and halt the violence.

Should a regime with an extremist, aggressive, and genocidal ideology come to power in the future, the presumptive case for nuclear rearmament by the United States even *before* that regime carried out a major attack would have to be considered. Genocide cannot be undone, and conventional invasions by an aggressor are much easier to prevent or deter than to roll back.

The Problem of Encouraging Proliferation

There is a fourth major challenge to the nuclear disarmament agenda—the very real risk that it could cause more harm than good on the nonproliferation front. This challenge is in many ways derivative of the three problems with the nuclear disarmament vision discussed above. But it merits separate attention, given its importance and the possibility that it could develop a dynamic of its own.

Many nuclear abolitionists are understandably motivated by what they see as the risk of accelerating proliferation of nuclear weapons around the world. Having watched Pakistan and India demonstrate their nuclear arsenals in the 1990s, North Korea do so the following decade, and Iran continue on its march toward a likely weapons capability, they are concerned that the process will not stop. Should it continue much longer, the norm against proliferation will weaken, and other countries that have been dissuaded in the past from getting the bomb may reconsider their options. If the sense develops that "everyone else is doing it" and that the penalties for building a bomb are modest in scale and scope, a snowballing process could begin. Moreover, the international community's current ability to stem this kind of tide is compromised by the existing nuclear arsenals of the major powers, which put them in an inherently inconsistent position when they argue against the pursuit of nuclear weapons by other states.

This logic about the risks of proliferation is correct in many ways. Indeed, it explains much of my motivation for supporting a nuclear disarmament regime that is viable and credible.

However, this logic also has a big problem. Regional nuclear proliferation could actually accelerate under the wrong approach to nuclear disarmament. Countries that now feel protected as a result of American extended deterrence could well begin to worry that the deterrent would weaken as the United States pursued the global elimination of nuclear weapons. Would the United States really come to their defense in a crisis, they might ask, if it had eliminated its nuclear weapons or was in the process of doing so? If nuclear disarmament was seen as having become the overarching goal of U.S. security policy, would anyone really believe that the United States would "risk Detroit to defend Dubai"? Perhaps the United States would no longer be seen as willing to respond with nuclear forces, if necessary, to an attack on its friends or allies abroad. And if it was not willing to respond with nuclear forces, even under extreme circumstances, the question would arise whether the United States would be willing to come to allies' defense with conventional forces alone. Conventional forces are time-consuming to mobilize and deploy, and their use often leads to protracted and bloody wars. Relying entirely on conventional capabilities may therefore not be as credible as current security arrangements. In such circumstances, allies would have powerful incentives to develop nuclear weapons of their own—even before a nuclear disarmament treaty was implemented and in fact possibly before it was even signed. This concern must be addressed now.

Key regional allies of the United States in turbulent parts of the world could be the first to feel the pressure to go nuclear (or, in Israel's case, to take existing capabilities "out of the closet"). The countries most likely to consider pursuing their own nuclear arsenals should the American deterrent seem to weaken might include Egypt, Iraq, Saudi Arabia, Turkey, and perhaps one or more smaller Gulf states, largely because of the perceived threat from Iran; Japan, South Korea, and Taiwan, mostly in light of their worries about China; and various neighbors of Russia. Similar pressures could arise in other parts of the world such as South America, where acquisition of the bomb by one major regional country could impel others to do the same. These American allies might worry that even as the United States and countries such as France and the United Kingdom got serious about giving up their arms, regional adversaries would find a way to circumvent any treaty restrictions. This concern is serious in light of the verification challenges outlined earlier. To be sure, any treaty abolishing nuclear weapons would become binding only once all parties were aboard. But making verification airtight would be hard, if not impossible.

Other worries could exist as well. A country like Iran led by a leader like Mahmoud Ahmadinejad might appear willing to develop and even use advanced biological arms. As argued earlier, that could worry the neighbors greatly if and when American nuclear weapons were no longer in existence, particularly if the biological threat were more potent than current agents. If the United States were to categorically renounce any possibility of ever using nuclear weapons in response to a biological attack, even a hugely lethal one, the problem of reduced deterrence and therefore reduced *assurance* of allies could manifest itself before a nuclear disarmament treaty even took effect.

An East Asian power might decide that, absent an American nuclear umbrella, it could no longer tolerate threats to its security from China's conventional military and should build its own bombs. Taiwan in particular might feel this way, given China's claims on the island and the lack of a formal security treaty between Taipei and Washington, but Japan and the Republic of Korea might reach such a conclusion as well. China has taken some steps to mitigate tensions in areas such as the South China Sea and East China Sea, and otherwise tried to reassure neighboring states about its intentions—although it has also taken some provocative actions, and its overall rise surely creates anxieties in a number of places in the region.[54] Upsetting the current state of affairs that has helped keep the peace in East Asia for decades is a risky proposition and needs to be carefully considered. Simple-minded pursuit of nuclear disarmament in such a situation may do more harm than good—even to the immediate nonproliferation agenda, if it makes leaders in Taipei or Seoul or Tokyo decide they better get the bomb just in case. Perhaps nuclear deterrence has been only a minor factor in preserving peace in the past; the issue is arguable. But policymakers need to be careful, and gradual, about how they run the experiment to test that proposition. An extended process of continuing to improve great-power relations, address sources of possible tension such as Taiwan, reduce nuclear arsenals, and reduce the salience of nuclear weapons in the security policies of key countries should precede a firm commitment to a nuclear disarmament accord.

Some advocates of nuclear disarmament downplay these kinds of concerns, arguing that they are somehow anachronistic, or not reflective of the true security challenges faced in key parts of the world today. In short, they argue that analysts and policymakers in the countries mentioned above are not worried about threats to their security under a nuclear disarmament regime or related treaty. This seems at most half the truth. To be sure, there are proponents of arms control around the world who would never argue for exercising their own country's future nuclear weapons options. But among U.S. allies are many leaders and policymakers who do worry acutely about the capabilities and intentions of their neighbors as well as about the smallest sign of a reduced American commitment to their security.

Previous attempts by international policymakers to show that history had fundamentally changed, and that the basic nature of interactions among nation-states had forever evolved, have been discredited in past eras. Policymakers must be careful to avoid making similar mistakes today. To be sure, prevailing realities of the international system can change with time; the prevalence of interstate war among great powers has been far less now for decades than its historical norm, and this may reflect a fundamental and durable shift. But to assume with ironclad confidence that it is permanent would be optimistic—and unprovable.

Maria Rublee, in her recent study of why many states have not chosen to pursue their own nuclear weapons, balanced the competing arguments and pressures nicely:

> The case studies provided persuasive evidence that we need a multitude of tools to discourage proliferation and encourage nuclear forbearance. Foreign intervention, great power pressure, and export controls hampered Egypt and Libya's nuclear programs, whereas security guarantees opened up enough policy space for conservatives in Japan, Sweden, and Germany to allow for nuclear abstinence. In short, realist measures made a difference. But in democratic countries, antinuclear peace groups leveraged the emerging international norm to strengthen their own position, making it too costly politically for conservatives to pursue a nuclear option.[55]

Countries such as Germany, Japan, and Sweden have not needed nuclear weapons, given the strength of U.S.-led security systems in their neighborhoods, among other factors. Political actors in each state favored nuclear weapons, but their motivations were ultimately seen as perhaps too nationalistic, or too autarkic, and the weapons were ultimately judged unnecessary under their specific circumstances.[56] Similar arguments could counter pronuclear weapons movements in other countries as well. But for countries less sure of their security, pursuing a nuclear weapon may seem a more reasonable recourse—and one less easily defeated by international pressure or lobbying.

Consider a bit more detail on several regional dynamics. Because my main purpose is to encourage greater care in how nuclear disarmament is pursued in general—with more conditions upon its enactment and more hedging about its future longevity than many now countenance—the approach need not be geographically comprehensive. The focus is therefore on two of the most important theaters, Northeast Asia and the broader Middle East.

Northeast Asia

At least three governments in this region might seriously consider acquiring nuclear weapons in the future: Japan, the Republic of Korea, and Taiwan. The future of the nuclear disarmament effort is only one factor that will affect any serious reconsideration of nuclear options by Tokyo, Seoul, and Taipei. But it is incumbent on proponents to frame the debate in a way that reduces the incentives of these governments to seek the bomb, or at least that does no net harm, rather than potentially increasing those incentives.

All three of these nations have had nuclear debates before; two of them, South Korea and Taiwan, have also had nuclear weapons programs in the past. And the degree of U.S. commitment to their security, including perceptions of the dependability of the American nuclear umbrella, has been important in their calculations. In short, when leaders sensed a weakening of the American commitment to help defend them, they were more inclined to initiate programs that could lead to production of their own nuclear bombs.

Japan has been fervently antinuclear ever since Hiroshima and Nagasaki were bombed in 1945. Since 1967 it has also adhered to a "three no" policy—pledging not to produce, possess, or introduce nuclear weapons. But Japan has also said over the years that it had the right to a nuclear weapon if needed for its own defense. One example is then–foreign minister Taro Aso, who said after the 2006 North Korean nuclear test that it was reasonable to debate the possibility of nuclear armament. Prominent think tanks, including one affiliated with former prime minister Yasuhiro Nakasone, have recently advocated keeping the nuclear option alive as well. The strength of the U.S. commitment to Japanese security and measures such as conventional military modernization and missile defense have been the main reasons that the antinuclear policy has remained firmly in place so far. Yet as a result of North Korean behavior and growing concerns about China, the antinuclear taboo in Japan has weakened somewhat over the years.[57]

A U.S. move toward nuclear disarmament that was seen as rash, rushed, or otherwise premature could be the decisive factor in causing Japan to reassess its nuclear choices. As a former Japanese prime minister, Morihiro Hosokawa, put it, "It is in the interest of the United States, so long as it does not wish to see Japan withdraw from the NPT and develop its own nuclear deterrent, to maintain its alliance with Japan and continue to provide a nuclear umbrella."[58] The prospect that Japan might go nuclear should not be exaggerated; a strong allergy to nuclear weapons remains in the country, and withdrawing from the NPT would complicate Japan's access to fuel needed for its nuclear energy program.[59] But under extreme circumstances, if the country felt vulnerable, ruling out the acquisition of nuclear weapons would be difficult.

Similar dynamics have been evident in both South Korea and Taiwan over the years. Each actually had a nuclear weapons program on two separate occasions in the past—and each time that program coincided with doubts about the U.S. commitment to its security. In Korea's case, the doubts were strongest in the 1970s, when a combination of the Vietnam War, differences of opinion over South Korean domestic governance, and other factors led Washington to create some distance in its dealings with Seoul. Seoul responded by seeking nuclear materials abroad in the early 1970s and then seeking the capacity to create its own materials later in the decade.[60] In more recent times North Korea's acquisition of a small nuclear arsenal has caused South Korea to worry. Defense Minister Yoon Kwang-ung requested assurances from the United States that it would respond in kind to any nuclear attack by Pyongyang against the Republic of Korea, and public opinion in South Korea at least temporarily favored development of an indigenous nuclear deterrent as well.[61]

In the case of Taiwan, the U.S. rapprochement with China in the 1980s led to a major nuclear weapons development effort. It was the second time such a program had been initiated—the first time being after China became a nuclear weapons state in 1964. In both cases Taiwan's interest was serious and involved construction of nuclear reactors designed to produce enough fissile material to build a modest nuclear arsenal along with some initial efforts at addressing related technical challenges such as reprocessing.[62]

Looking ahead, it is very difficult to predict confidently how Koreans and Taiwanese will see their future interest in nuclear capabilities. If the peninsula were someday reunified, the Republic of Korea could inherit North Korea's nuclear arsenal, as one plausible scenario (in addition to retaining all the nuclear technology and materials that are within its own extensive civilian nuclear power program). It would then have to wrestle with its own views about its role in the future international security order in a part of the world where several major states already have nuclear weapons programs. Its degree of confidence in American security commitments and its comfort level with that dependence would presumably be important factors in decisionmaking, if basic logic and South Korean history are guides.[63]

Taiwan could face such questions even more acutely, given China's claims on its territory combined with growing Chinese conventional military capabilities. Taiwan probably could use spent fuel from its nuclear reactors to build a bomb fairly quickly— perhaps within a year or less. That it will do so anytime soon is doubtful, given China's past threats that such a development could be a *causus belli* and the likelihood of strong American objections. As Derek Mitchell put it, "although Taiwan may view a nuclear option as insurance against possible future U.S. abandonment, such a program could make this scenario a self-fulfilling prophecy." But that calculation could change in the event that leaders in Taipei saw the United States as having already reduced its commitment to Taiwan's defense.[64]

The Broader Middle East

With Israel already possessing a nuclear weapons capability, Pakistan on the fringes of the region now holding one, Syria apparently having had nuclear ambitions at least until Israel's 2007 air strike set them back, and Iran likely headed toward a nuclear weapons option, the issue of how countries in this region will assess their nuclear choices in the future is also crucial.

Egypt pursued nuclear weapons in the 1960s and early 1970s before abandoning the effort. Saudi Arabia is suspected by some to have certain understandings with nuclear-armed Pakistan about possible access to its arsenal, or military help from Pakistani forces that could deploy with nuclear arms in their possession, in the event of an acute crisis. But in the end neither Egypt nor Saudi Arabia appears to have been determined to pay the sustained budgetary or political costs associated with a decision to build its own arsenal. Turkey's position may be slightly murkier. But Ankara does not currently appear strongly inclined to reconsider its nuclear option.[65]

Especially given Iran's behavior, all these assessments could be contingent on continuation of a robust American security commitment to the region, however. To date that commitment has seemed self-evident to most, particularly in light of the decisive U.S. military actions this decade in Iraq. But talk of nuclear abolition could cause worries. Former U.S. ambassador to Israel Martin Indyk and Tamara Wittes have worried that even with a continued American role in the region and continued U.S. retention of a large and flexible nuclear force, additional explicit security guarantees might be required for regional security partners should Iran acquire a bomb.[66] Indyk and Wittes have spoken of a more explicit extension of an American nuclear umbrella over the region, rather than leaving vague the circumstances under which the United States would respond in kind to any Iranian nuclear attack against its friends. Because Saudi Arabia and other members of the Gulf Cooperation Council are American friends and security partners but not formal allies, such a measure might be seen as especially important by some. Historical and economic ties between the United States and Saudi Arabia, for example, would seem to suggest a strong security commitment, but the fact that fifteen of the 9/11 hijackers came from Saudi Arabia as well as other strains in the relationship make some worry that informal commitments may not be enough.[67]

Conclusion

Beyond these issues—questions of verifiability, deterring advanced biological attack, recognizing the limits of conventional military power, and avoiding undesired regional security dynamics that actually increase proliferation risks in the short term—the goal of global nuclear disarmament faces other major impediments. Notably, several other existing nuclear weapons states can be expected to object to the idea even more strongly than the United States would. Their positions may change over time—after all, countries such as Argentina, Brazil, Libya, South Africa, and Ukraine have abandoned bomb programs or even relinquished nuclear arsenals in the past, when their governments or their basic incentives and national priorities have changed.[68] But right now the challenge is considerable.

Russia is the lead case in point, given its large land mass and long borders to defend, as well as its shaky economy and declining population. It has for years reserved the right to use nuclear weapons first in a conflict and shows few signs of changing that policy.[69]

Israel is another example. Perhaps it would forgo its existing nuclear arsenal if a comprehensive Mideast peace deal combined with verifiable and lasting proof of Iranian nuclear disarmament were achieved.[70] But the challenges are immense. And they do not revolve only around Iranian president Ahmadinejad, who is adamantly opposed to the very existence of the Jewish state and whose attitudes thereby pose a fundamental reason why Israel will continue to worry greatly about its security for many years to come.[71] In addition, in the words of several notable Russian scholars, "the authoritarian nature of the majority of Islamic regimes and the growth of fundamentalism and radicalism in the Greater Middle East would not allow Israel to rely fully on the inviolability of agreements with neighboring countries, without having some kind of military 'insurance policy,' including nuclear weapons." Indeed, the same authors conclude that even hypothetical U.S. nuclear guarantees and Israeli membership in NATO would not suffice; their best idea "could be the partial dismantling of nuclear warheads and their storage in a non-operationally-ready (separated) state under international oversight, with the understanding that if Israel felt the threat of aggression, it could fairly quickly reassemble its nuclear deterrent."[72] In any event, Israel is likely to be extremely reluctant to eliminate its nuclear weapons for a very long time to come.[73] In this light, it was probably unfortunate that the most significant initiative of the 2010 Non-Proliferation Treaty Review Conference in New York was to call for negotiations on creating a nuclear-free Middle East. There could be some benefits to such talks if they are adroitly handled, such as forcing more regional states effectively to acknowledge Israel.[74] But the prospects for realization of the stated objective of the negotiations would seem mediocre at best.

Even a country like Great Britain has resisted disarmament. When he was prime minister, Tony Blair made an impassioned statement against the idea. In defending his decision to modernize the force, Blair argued that his critics "would need to prove that such a gesture [British unilateral disarmament] would change the minds of hardliners and extremists in countries which are developing these nuclear capabilities. They would need to show that terrorists would be less likely to conspire against us with hostile governments because we had given up our nuclear weapons."[75] In the end, both Britain and France could well be open to a nuclear disarmament debate under the right circumstances—but a good deal would have to change in their national strategic thinking first.[76]

4 DISMANTLING, NOT ABOLISHING, NUCLEAR WEAPONS

SO NUCLEAR WEAPONS WOULD seem too dangerous to keep, yet impossible to eliminate. Is there a way out of this paradox?

The answer is yes, if the goal is the dismantlement of nuclear weapons rather than their permanent extinction. Abolition is too sweeping, absolute, and permanent an action. The force of a treaty alone will not relegate nuclear weapons to the dustbin of history. But complete dismantlement for an indefinite period may be possible. Depending on the course of human history, disarmament may wind up being a lasting reality—but that will be a determination for future generations to make.

The ambitiousness of most nuclear abolitionists is commendable in one sense. Thinking big is needed to contemplate something so dramatic as the elimination of a whole class of weapons given the long conflict-ridden history of the human race. But modesty is also needed. No treaty can be designed to guarantee that once nuclear weapons and fissile materials are eliminated, the situation will endure. Only by recognizing the limits of what can be achieved through a decision made in the twenty-first century can policymakers make that ambitious accomplishment possible. The world's leaders must think big, but not too big; they should dream, and use their imaginations, but not move into the realm of fantasy.

A practical case, discussed below, can be made against rushing to action. Even under conditions in which one could imagine pursuing a treaty regime purposefully and energetically, a serious case can be made against believing that any such accord should be viewed as necessarily permanent.

We can and should aspire to a world without any deployed and ready-to-use nuclear weapons—better yet, a world without any assembled nuclear weapons or separated and bomb-ready fissile materials. But a world of zero weapons should not be confused with a world in which nuclear weapons have been abolished for good. Depending on the future course of history, these weapons may be needed again. I thus spend more time than have most previous authors describing a strategy for realistic reconstitution of nuclear weapons. This approach might be called a hawkish vision of nuclear disarmament. But in my view, it is the only viable approach if the concept of nuclear disarmament is to be beneficial to the security of the United States and its many allies and friends around the world.

The idea here is not to create a faux regime that would allow the United States or any other country to easily reverse its commitment to nuclear disarmament. It is rather a simple recognition that nuclear disarmament may not last forever, at least not continuously. Periods of nuclear dismantlement and disarmament may be occasionally interrupted by one or more temporary periods of reconstitution to contain crises that have erupted because of the aggressive actions of a dangerous state. Only by recognizing this point can policymakers ensure that the treaty will do more good than harm. Only with this awareness can skeptical countries and worried partners of the United States be convinced to join in pursuit of the vision of eliminating nuclear weapons—rather than consider developing their own bombs. Only in this way can policymakers also signal to would-be violators of any such treaty that the international community has not gone soft on security or grown isolationist in attitude—that it retains the will and the means to respond firmly, swiftly, and effectively to any treaty violation.

This chapter first discusses the issue of timing—when, and under what conditions, will it make sense to pursue a nuclear zero accord. Second, the chapter describes several practical aspects of any disarmament regime concerning matters such as verification, building largely on the excellent work already done by others on the topic. Third, it considers the issue of reconstitution, describing how the United States and perhaps other countries might temporarily exit from a nuclear disarmament regime should circumstances warrant. These three elements of a nuclear disarmament regime—when to pursue it, how to implement it, and how to allow for its temporary suspension if necessary—are in fact equally important. It may seem paradoxical that a large fraction of the architecture of a nuclear disarmament regime should be devoted to explaining the conditions under which the regime would be suspended. That is not common in the history of arms control. But nuclear disarmament is not like other incremental, iterative arms control—it is a sweeping decision to try to eliminate the most lethal weapons ever known to man, and its radical quality must not be underestimated.

Timing the Treaty

Many proponents of a nuclear disarmament accord want to move to a treaty within a decade or so. They may acknowledge that time will be needed to convince relatively stable countries like Russia, as well as irresponsible countries like Iran and North Korea, to abandon their weapons. Nonetheless, these advocates still aspire to a time line in which negotiations on a treaty would begin within ten years, with the global elimination of nuclear weapons ideally to occur by 2030 or 2035.

Many foreign policy traditionalists and practitioners agree on the desirability of a denuclearized world in the abstract but do not favor moving toward it anytime soon, even aspirationally. (Yet another group believes the bomb may do more good than harm and in any case see no plausible path to its elimination at any point.) The implicit strategy among those who aspire to nuclear disarmament but consider it very far off might be described as trying to build a more peaceful and prosperous world now and worrying about an issue like eliminating nuclear weapons from the planet later. They might argue that, after all, since 1945 the world has seen remarkable progress on a variety of fronts. Great-power war has effectively ended; with the demise of communism, great ideological struggles have largely ended as well—especially since violent Islamic extremists are in fact not popular within the broader Muslim world. The case for optimism is not airtight, and a more peaceful international environment is not a predetermined outcome, but the natural path toward a safer world may not require implementation of radical ideas like abolishing nuclear weapons. Continuing to resolve key regional conflicts, locking in great-power cooperation on issues like energy policy and trade policy, and building new and stronger multilateral structures of governance like the European Union and the Group of Twenty (G-20) may be the best path ahead for now. Dramatic ideas like banishing a whole class of weapons can, by this interpretation, wait for the day when war between all major states becomes just as unthinkable as war would be today within the European Union or NATO or the broader Western alliance. Come the twenty-second century or so, the world may be ready for such a step.

In my estimation, a middle-ground position makes the most sense. Moving to a nuclear disarmament now, by trying to write a treaty in the next few years, is too fast, but dropping the subject and waiting for the twenty-second century is too slow. Trying to abolish nuclear weapons too soon could undercut U.S. allies who worry about how they will ensure their security in a dangerous world. It could weaken deterrent arrangements that are working today but that are also somewhat fragile. And it could encourage extremist states to build up nuclear arsenals as existing nuclear powers build down. It also lacks credibility in a world in which even some responsible countries have no interest in denuclearizing anytime soon. Absent a serious process for moving toward zero, declaration of ambitious but arbitrary and unattainable deadlines for action is more likely to discredit the nuclear disarmament agenda than to advance it.[1]

Putting off the nuclear disarmament agenda creates its own substantial problems, however. It leaves existing powers in a weak position to form coalitions to pressure would-be proliferators to forgo nuclear weapons. It fosters a false sense of security and complacency about the supposed safety of living with the bomb.

The United States should endorse a nuclear-free world with conviction, as President Obama did in his 2009 Prague speech. But for the foreseeable future, it should not work to create a treaty and should not sign any treaty that others might create.

The timing of a nuclear disarmament agenda should not be set to a calendar. Rather, the right time horizon for seriously pushing a new nuclear accord is after most of the world's half dozen or so key territorial and existential issues involving major powers are resolved.[2] As discussed below, and previously in chapter 3, these issues include the status of Taiwan; the matter of Kashmir; political relations between Russia and key "near-abroad" states, Georgia and Ukraine in particular; and the Arab-Israeli conflict. (Nuclear crises involving Iran and North Korea also need to be addressed, although the beginnings of a move toward nuclear disarmament might not have to await their complete resolution.) Once these contentious matters are largely resolved, the plausibility of great-power war over any imaginable issue that one can identify today will be very low. That in turn will make the basic structure and functioning of the international political system stable enough to take the risk of moving toward a nuclear-free world—a process that will be so radical as to be inherently destabilizing in some sense and thus prudent to pursue only when the great powers are in a cooperative mode and undivided by irredentist territorial issues.

With luck, most of those issues can be successfully addressed in the next couple of decades. But we cannot know that yet.

Regardless, now is the time to start thinking about a nuclear disarmament treaty, even if now is not yet the time to start negotiating it. The prospect of such an accord can help existing nuclear powers rebut claims by the likes of Iran and North Korea that they are hypocritical. Teheran, Pyongyang, and others implicitly or explicitly tend to argue that established nuclear powers have no business denying others the full range of nuclear options when they insist on holding onto nuclear weapons themselves. Extremist regimes will find other ways to complain, of course, and they will not be impressed by the global move toward denuclearization. But they will lose a key excuse in the eyes of many other states about why they are supposedly within their rights in pursuing the bomb or dual-use technologies such as uranium enrichment centrifuges that could facilitate acquisition of the bomb.[3] In addition, the nuclear disarmament issue is now squarely on the international agenda, thanks to the efforts of key nuclear disarmament advocates such as Henry Kissinger, George Shultz, William Perry, and Sam Nunn, not to mention President Obama. That means the vision of a nuclear-free world is already in play, and already can be a force for good, or for harm, to the international security order. Finally, active dialogue over a potential treaty can encourage research about various complex matters of verification and related issues and otherwise influence near-term arms control efforts, at least at the margin.

Why should negotiation of a global nuclear disarmament treaty await improvement of great-power relations and resolution of most of the main potential causes of crisis or war among them? It is because the process of moving toward zero will be disruptive to deterrent relationships that are currently working rather well. Fundamentally altering these dynamics should not be done carelessly or prematurely.

Consider several specific cases. In recent years scholars at Brookings have carried out simulations of Taiwan crisis scenarios with colleagues from the East Asia region. I have been struck by the care and caution with which the participants tend to approach their decisions in these artificial crises—not unlike what leaders have tended to do in the real world in recent decades. A culture of professionalism and prudence has been established in dealing with such problems, on all sides. A sort of semi-safe zone of crisis diplomacy has been established within an admittedly still unstable and fragile situation. It is important that the situation be solved, that Taiwan's future status not be confused and disputed forever. But a rush toward a nuclear disarmament outcome that leaves parties doubting their previous partnerships and power positions could be harmful in this context. Indeed, because many Chinese view the Taiwan issue as a matter of vital national interest for their country, some Chinese scholars and officials have raised the possibility that China might use nuclear weapons during a Taiwan conflict.[4] The risks could increase in a world in which reduced U.S. nuclear force levels approached those of China.

A similar conclusion can be reached regarding Russia. Consider the August 2008 war in Georgia, initiated by ethnic and border disputes in South Ossetia and Abkhazia. Russian tanks were marching on the Georgian capital within days and might have overthrown President Mikheil Saakashvili. But the Bush administration's threat of unspecified yet serious reprisals seems to have helped cool things off, and Russia stopped its menacing moves toward Tbilisi. Few believed that any American nuclear threat, or even conventional military response, was in the offing. But a certain cautiousness prevailed nonetheless, at least after an initial period of carelessness on the part of both Russians and Georgians, which helped produce the conflict in the first place. Were nuclear weapons really important in preventing an escalation of the crisis? Probably not. But could things have been different if, during this crisis, Russia and the United States were denuclearizing? Might one side have felt pressure to escalate the crisis to prove that it still had ample mettle and resolve even without the traditional trappings of superpower nuclear capability? Inserting a radical disarmament agenda into this situation might be smart if the world were somehow being dragged right to the brink of apocalypse already by these kinds of small border disputes within the former Soviet space. On the other hand, it seems more likely that the predominant patterns of caution built up over more than half a century continue to exert a tempering effect on possible conflicts. Such patterns of caution are something to be retained, rather than risked, as long as the general regional trend is moving in a stabilizing direction.

As a practical matter, Russia probably views these stabilizing aspects of the current nuclear balance as being even more important than does the United States. Russia's long land borders heighten the salience of the territorial defense mission for its armed forces, but the decline of its military forces underscores the difficulty of achieving that mission with conventional forces alone. Russia will probably not truly support the nuclear disarmament vision until it feels a great deal more secure in its strategic position than it does today.[5]

Other problems too could pit the United States against either China or Russia, even in this day and age, such as disputes between China and America's ally Japan over seabed resources. Seeing progress on this matter would itself be desirable before an energetic pursuit of a nuclear disarmament accord was undertaken.

Matters that involve smaller regional powers may themselves be enough to impede any realistic path to nuclear disarmament. These include, notably, the Kashmir dispute between India and Pakistan.[6] Perhaps it is possible to imagine a world in which conventional military deterrence proves adequate to manage any major regional tensions that occur. Given current realities, however, pursuing nuclear disarmament is too much right now.

The chances that Iran or North Korea would go along with any verification regime seem slight. The chances that they would make a sincere commitment to forgo nuclear weapons seem low in light of the extreme politics each regime pursues. The difficulty of responding to a possible nuclear threat by either with American conventional military forces, and those of any willing coalition partners, is not unthinkable, but it is greater than many realize. And there is the worry, small but real, that such states might transfer nuclear weapons to terrorists. Defense Secretary Robert Gates took this threat seriously enough in October 2008 to suggest a possible broadening of the United States' nuclear deterrence doctrine, pledging to hold "fully accountable" any country or group that helped terrorists obtain or employ weapons of mass destruction.[7] For these and other reasons, the likelihood of a serious move toward nuclear disarmament being welcomed today by American allies in the neighborhood of Iran or North Korea is low. And the potential for perverse, counterproductive effects that could actually *encourage* U.S. allies to seek their own nuclear arsenals is great indeed.

This line of reasoning should not be pushed too far. If nuclear weapons can be eliminated only when no risks of interstate conflict exist anywhere on the planet, a utopian state would be required for disarmament. But putting nuclear disarmament first and resolution of disputes second on key regional issues over which bloody wars have been fought before, and over which American allies find their interests heavily engaged and their very survival to be at stake is a dubious proposition. Again, the act of disarmament is an inherently disruptive process that calls into doubt the stability and dependability of previous deterrent relationships; if those relationships are generally working, they should be put at risk only very carefully and thoughtfully. At a bare minimum, most remaining serious regional problems should be resolved before a treaty is negotiated—particularly existential matters involving American allies. The security relationships among the great powers must improve substantially before a nuclear disarmament regime would make much sense.

If the list of major international disputes can be reduced to just one or two, perhaps a nuclear disarmament accord could be negotiated and readied for implementation—but not fully carried out. This approach might help the international community gain additional leverage over whichever recalcitrant nuclear states were trying to retain their weapons or failing to resolve their major disputes with neighbors. That is possible, although it is too soon to know now, and much would depend on the specifics of the case. But given the large number of existing disputes, including some that could directly pit major powers against each other, the dangers of unintended consequences loom too large to pursue nuclear disarmament anytime soon.

Design and Implementation

But someday, perhaps within two to three decades, many or even all of the above issues may be solved. At that time, a treaty could be pursued. The treaty would have to be a fairly complex.

A nuclear disarmament accord would require that all existing nuclear weapons and weapons-grade fissile material in all countries possessing nuclear capabilities be catalogued and then eliminated. The accord would require ongoing monitoring of all major nuclear facilities, notably power reactors and their supporting fuel-cycle industries, wherever they exist around the world. It would also allow for challenge inspections in cases of suspected cheating, with mechanisms such as automatic economic sanctions that could be applied to any country found cheating or unwilling to accept the additional monitoring.[8]

Nuclear weapons would be banned. No state would have the right to posses them. Materials designed for use in them would no longer be produced. Ideally, highly enriched uranium (HEU) would no longer be used even in research reactors and submarines and would no longer exist. Plutonium would not be separated from reactor waste for use as a fuel because any process that carried out such extraction could be quickly modified to produce bomb-grade material. Existing stocks of plutonium would ideally be consumed as fuel in future reactors, rather than stored in ways that might allow plutonium to be reclaimed for future bomb use. Facilities designed to enrich uranium to low levels for reactor use and to process radioactive waste in preparation for disposal would be closely monitored and perhaps multilaterally owned and operated. Uranium mines might be monitored. To reduce the number of facilities requiring monitoring as well as the number of places having latent nuclear weapons production facilities, larger (and preferably democratic, open) countries or an international fuel bank might offer subsidized fuel to countries wishing to have nuclear power.

In short, the goal would be to keep close watch on all nuclear facilities, to prohibit production and retention of fissile material (or dedicated bomb components) usable in a nuclear device, and thereby to have at least months of advance warning of any decision by any state to pursue a nuclear weapon. There would be no double standards on verification or anything else for that matter; all nuclear facilities in all places would be treated comparably.[9] For that reason, even democratic countries would need to accept the occasional challenge inspection on their territory, simply to preserve a sense of fair play and equality under the regime.

Nuclear-capable delivery vehicles might be limited in number.[10] But bans would not be practical. Bombers and other combat aircraft would still be needed for conventional weapons purposes, as would certain types of submarines. Long-range ballistic missiles might be restricted in number, but their inherent similarities to space-launch vehicles would make outright bans impractical. Cruise missiles would also still exist. As a result, constraints on delivery vehicles might complement bans on warheads and fissile materials and could limit, perhaps, the aggregate size of a country's rapid-strike nuclear breakout force. But they could not constitute a robust means of ensuring compliance.

A treaty would take effect only after all nuclear-weapons-owning states signed and ratified it. Indeed, its complete implementation would have to await signature and ratification by all states having any nuclear facilities to speak of, for reasons noted above. Implementation could take place over several years and allow for periodic reviews so that states could gain additional confidence in each other's compliance with the terms of the accord.

A strong international watchdog and monitoring agency would be charged with the verification effort during the initial implementation period and thereafter. Its budget would surely exceed $1 billion a year, based on analogy with existing inspection systems. The funding level for today's International Atomic Energy Agency (IAEA) is somewhat more than $100 million a year.[11] But the current IAEA has failed to detect activities such as the Iranian uranium enrichment facility at Qom and the Syrian nuclear reactor project (subsequently destroyed by Israel in 2007).[12] And its purview is limited to a much more narrow set of sites than would be necessary under a nuclear disarmament regime.

Some believe that a nuclear disarmament accord would have to preclude states from the right of subsequent withdrawal.[13] That may or may not be constitutional in the U.S. system. My view is that the option of withdrawal—or at least of temporarily reconstituting a nuclear arsenal—would have to be integral to the nuclear disarmament treaty. More is said on this below.

Many advocates of abolition favor near-term steps that could precede a nuclear disarmament treaty. They advocate ratification of the comprehensive nuclear test ban treaty; cessation of production of fissile materials for weapons purposes; conversion of reactors currently employing highly enriched uranium to use low-enriched uranium (LEU); voluntary acceptance of the IAEA "additional protocol," meaning granting the agency the right to monitor not only nuclear reactors but also other sensitive sites and some locations where nuclear-related activities are suspected; further cuts in existing nuclear arsenals; and creation of binding nuclear-weapon-free zones. These steps are generally sound, but one other common proposal on the near-term policy agenda of abolitionists—nuclear no-first-use pledges—is to my mind more problematic.[14]

One particularly useful near-term proposal comes from Graham Allison of Harvard, who convincingly advocates a dedicated global alliance to create a "Fort Knox" security standard for fissile materials in the years before a nuclear disarmament treaty could be implemented. His approach would require countries not only to allow systematic monitoring by outside bodies but also to enhance their own systems of safeguards and protections. He would also have them create a fund to help less wealthy countries improve their internal security practices. Allison would clamp down on proliferation as well—criminalizing violations of export control regimes, as well as creating international bodies to oversee an effort to tighten those controls and track the behavior of possible proliferators.[15]

The verification task would be daunting for reasons outlined in chapter 3. Fissile materials are fairly plentiful, and even more than that, they are inherently hard to detect. Only short-range sensors operating in close proximity to uranium or plutonium have any real hope of finding even unshielded materials. And nothing about the laws of physics or the course of technology suggests this situation will change. One can imagine a fairly airtight monitoring system for each and every major declared nuclear facility; detection technologies probably are good enough to make such observation methods effective. But the simple fact that existing stocks of fissile materials are not completely accounted for means that tracking down all small amounts of material will be very hard. The United States and Russia might not be capable of finding *their own* complete inventories, let alone working through an international agency to find someone else's.[16] That said, the problem becomes less daunting if one simply accepts that airtight verification will not and cannot be the cornerstone on which a nuclear disarmament regime is built. This is not to argue for lax inspections or tolerance of slippage in countries' obligations to come completely clean on their nuclear obligations. It is rather a recognition of reality. It guides much of the rest of my own concept for nuclear disarmament, developed below.

Reconstitution

The capacity to make nuclear weapons is a permanent attribute of modern human civilization. No treaty can change it. Especially in a world that relies on nuclear power for energy, the materials needed for making bombs as well as the knowledge needed to fashion them into explosive devices will always be readily and widely available. Mankind's capacity for reconstitution, even after the complete elimination of nuclear weapons, is therefore a fact of life that will not change. No concept for nuclear disarmament can refute this fact. For these and other reasons, nuclear abolition is unrealistic and probably impossible, if the term abolition is taken to mean the absolute, verifiable, and permanent elimination of nuclear weapons with complete confidence that they can never return.

So any nuclear disarmament regime must address the question of reconstitution. The bomb can always be rebuilt, whether one likes that fact or not. In my view, however, that ability to rebuild is an asset in the pursuit of nuclear disarmament, not a liability. No one can now know if the complete and permanent elimination of nuclear weapons is feasible or, compared with other possible threats and dangers that could emerge, even desirable. Thankfully, no one needs to figure this out. What is needed is a way to rebuild arsenals quickly and dependably—and transparently and legitimately—if that is ever required. As long as a way can be found to do so that is credible in advance, and impossible for would-be enemies to prevent, the international community will have a much more practical path to eliminating American and allied nuclear weapons than if it had to devise in 2020 or 2030 a future global regime that was required to last until not just 2050 but until 2100, 2200, and beyond. No one is either that wise or that clairvoyant, but the right concept for global nuclear disarmament can make a virtue of this fact and view the elimination of nuclear weapons as a provisional measure, reversible if need be.

One hopes, of course, that reconstitution will never be necessary. Ideally, once eliminated, nuclear weapons will no longer seem to have any place in world politics, and the state of the international system will continue to stabilize so that severe future challenges will be unlikely—especially from state-on-state violence. In that world, what is designed as a reversible measure might evolve into a de facto permanent reality. But that will be for future generations to decide.

Various questions must be considered in any strategy for reconstitution that would be motivated by detection of cheating (or other horrendous action) by a key party to the nuclear disarmament treaty:

—What body would justify and legitimate any decision to rebuild a small arsenal?

—Would an individual country do the rebuilding, or an international group?

—How clear would the evidence of violation by another state have to be to justify the rearmament?

—Would any action besides documented proof of nuclear rearmament by one state be grounds for the United States (or another state) to reconstitute?

—What kinds of materials and facilities would be allowable under a nuclear disarmament accord, as a hedging strategy?

The decision to reconstitute begins with the need to face reality: if it truly feels threatened, no state will wait very long for approval from an international body like the UN Security Council to rebuild a nuclear arsenal.[17] Reconstitution mechanisms therefore need to be fast and simple. If they are not, the system will not be credible. In addition, for a key country like the United States, onerous legal demands for justifying rearmament could cause great worries for its allies. They might then doubt its ability to rearm in time to protect them from a threat in their vicinities. Their own willingness to accept global nuclear disarmament will thereby decline, and even American allies may wind up opposing the concept—or secretly pursuing closet nuclear bomb programs despite their formal obligations not to do so.

At the same time, countries cannot be permitted to recreate nuclear arsenals at the slightest provocation or without due cause. Nor can they be allowed simply to cite their own intelligence estimates that another state is potentially cheating on its disarmament obligations as sufficient grounds for rearming. The experience of the Iraq war, in which faulty American intelligence was a major basis for justifying the conflict that began in 2003, will remain fresh in many minds for a long time. Although some blame the cynicism of the Bush administration, or even its purported dishonesty, for that intelligence failure, in fact much of the problem resulted from the inherent difficulty of knowing what another state is doing within its own borders and its own weapons laboratories, together with methodological mistakes by intelligence professionals.[18] In short, similar intelligence failures could occur again. For example, better international intelligence cooperation on tracking suspicious trading in high technology goods that could be used in a nuclear weapons program—a good idea, to be sure[19]—could nonetheless wind up producing a "false positive." It would be a great shame if a nuclear disarmament regime fell apart because one state's fears that another was rearming led it to rearm too—especially if in the end those intelligence reports turned out to be wrong.

As discussed in an earlier chapter, biological arms could pose a complex challenge too. If a serious pathogen was developed for offensive purposes by a given country and then discovered, the question whether it was a sufficiently egregious violation of the Biological Weapons Convention to justify another state withdrawing from the nuclear disarmament regime would be crucially important and very difficult. A nuclear disarmament treaty should clarify that only biological weapons with likely potential lethal effects comparable to those of nuclear weapons should be viewed as sufficient grounds for legitimate withdrawal as a response. This approach would still leave room for interpretation, and controversy, but there is probably no other viable approach that can be written out in general terms ahead of time.[20]

Even an extremely threatening conventional military buildup by one state could justify action by others. It is hard to be precise on this point, unfortunately, but certainly a doubling in conventional military power—measured in the relative growth of defense spending by comparison with neighbors, or the size of armed forces—over, say, a decade would be noteworthy. If the country's neighbors were not embarked on a buildup themselves, the cause for concern would grow. If the buildup was accompanied by a hostile or aggressive ideology on the part of the governing regime, the case would be even stronger. Clearly, a conventional military buildup by one country should lead to a nuclear rearmament effort by another only under extreme circumstances. But these situations cannot be entirely precluded.

If violations of the nuclear disarmament regime are suspected, the evidence should be presented and discussed at the UN Security Council. But at the same time, the decision of other states to rearm in response will not and cannot require full consensus even among the core members of the Security Council. This is especially true if one of them is the source of the initial problem, but it applies regardless.

So we have a dilemma. Depending on the UN Security Council for authorization to rearm requires too high a burden of proof on the country or countries suspecting treaty violations and potentially slows down, dangerously, the response to any violation. But allowing individual states to reach their own decisions risks allowing faulty intelligence or politics to undermine the nuclear disarmament regime.

This problem has no perfect solution. The best compromise could be a contact group for each country that wishes to preserve the right to build or rebuild a nuclear arsenal under extreme conditions. The contact group would not have binding decisionmaking power, but it would ensure that the evidence being used to justify nuclear rearmament was well debated before the rearming country took any action. It would also provide the broader international community with a range of informed views.

The contact group for the United States might consist of a small group of countries that enjoy some distance from Washington in the eyes of the international community, yet are also friendly enough to the United States to take its security concerns seriously. Such a group of about ten states might include Australia, Britain, Canada, France, Germany, and Japan, for example, as well as generally friendly but somewhat more neutral states such as Brazil, India, Indonesia, and the Philippines. Again, this group would not have veto power over a U.S. decision to rearm, but Washington would agree in advance to give them ample opportunity to understand the sources of its concern, reach their own assessments, and discuss these assessments publicly. This approach would provide an extra layer of checks and balances, beyond the transparency gained by a partially open UN Security Council debate.

Any other power that might be a likely candidate to build an arsenal in the future should make a similar political commitment to create a contact group of trusted yet independent-minded states with which it would consult before rebuilding an arsenal—as an additional transparency measure and additional check and balance. For a country like Russia with a strong history of state secrecy, creating a meaningful and effective contact group could be even harder than for the United States. But any country's initial roster of contact group states, as well as any subsequent revisions to the group that occurred thereafter, could be presented and discussed internationally to discourage a country from stacking the deck entirely with dependable foreign regimes.

Any decision to reconstitute should be the beginning and not the end of a process of international consultation and monitoring. If, for example, the United States, strongly suspecting a nuclear weapons (or an advanced biological weapons or egregious conventional military) program in a hostile state, decided to act even in the absence of formal UN Security Council approval, it would need to do more than simply share initial suspicions with the United Nations and consult with its contact group. Once a reconstitution effort began, international monitoring would be required—with the goal of seeing that any rebuilt arsenal was transparent to the international community. A state unwilling to accept this, or a state believed by others to be making a fundamentally indefensible decision to reconstitute an arsenal, could be subject to the same international sanctions that the original violator would presumably suffer, as discussed below. No inspectors from the country initially suspected of violating the treaty would be included, of course. And it might even be necessary to prevent the monitors from knowing exactly where they were geographically, to preclude preventive strikes by the violating country against specific locations in the rearming state. But steps should be taken to share information to the extent possible.

Any state responding to a foreboding international development by rebuilding an arsenal should be expected to do so only as a temporary measure. Reconstitution would not be permanent, even if it might last years or even decades. The nuclear disarmament regime should be seen as permanent even if there were one or more times in the future of the human race when nuclear weapons were rebuilt for a stretch.

Some would argue for international control of any such recon-stituted arsenal, building on earlier ideas from the dawn of the nuclear era such as the Baruch plan. But that notion seems far-fetched, in a world in which governance and security still are gen-erally provided by nation states. Leave aside the possibility that a violating country might try to wreak havoc with any multilateral arrangement, directly or through proxies. The detection of a vio-lation of the nuclear disarmament treaty would cause consider-able worry about the most fundamental interests of countries that might be threatened by the violator. It would not be the time, or the issue, to promote aspirations of global governance. It would be the moment to ensure reliable national security for the United States and its close allies.

Again, the process for promoting a nuclear disarmament regime—and addressing any future challenges to it—must be credible. Even today, in preliminary discussions of the notion, it is important to get such details right. Otherwise, even tentative American pursuit of a nuclear disarmament agenda could cause great angst among allies who could wonder if an idealistic or utopian streak in U.S. national security thinking was emerging—one that could potentially jeopardize their long-term security by weakening deterrence and perhaps emboldening adversaries. The kind of serious scenarios at issue here would go far beyond the kinds of violations of arms control accords that the United States worried the Soviet Union could commit during the cold war. Those were violations of degree. But secretly building nuclear weapons, or advanced biological arms, after everyone else in the world had eliminated theirs would be violation of kind, a funda-mental challenge not just to this arms control regime but to the existing international order. It would conjure up great concerns about the underlying intentions of any country guilty of ignoring a sacred trust to other states. It would require the most serious and firm of responses.

Automatic sanctions have been suggested as an element of any nuclear disarmament accord, to deter violations of the treaty by making it clear to all that meaningful consequences would automatically result from cheating. Such ideas make sense and should be written into the treaty—perhaps up to and including bans on trade in all high-technology goods with the offending state as well as broader and more sweeping economic penalties such as high across-the-board tariffs. Other steps could also be envisioned such as expelling the offending state from all international organizations.[21] Certainly it is possible to be much tougher with these sorts of measures than required by existing rules under the Non-Proliferation Treaty, whether for a nuclear disarmament regime or less ambitious approaches to stemming proliferation.[22]

But however these ideas are tweaked, they will not suffice. One reason is that automatic sanctions might not be implemented for lack of certainty about intelligence concerning the suspect state's weapons programs. Even if the sanctions were in some sense automatic, they would still need to be triggered, and unless a smoking gun were found—or the nuclear disarmament implementation agency booted out of the offending country—evidence might be insufficient to allow a clear triggering.

The problem is in fact even more serious and fundamental. Sanctions might simply not suffice as a response given the stakes involved. A country that decided, for example, to build nuclear or advanced biological weapons for itself when no other state had them, after having previously sworn to abide by regimes outlawing the technologies, must be presumed to be very dangerous. Perhaps its interest in such weapons of mass destruction would be relatively benign and motivated more by paranoia than aggressive intent. But it must be presumed that a violation could in fact amount to a very foreboding development, the initial steps of a regime bent on conquering neighbors or at least seizing disputed territories. Perhaps the cheating state would try to blackmail the international community to concede it various natural resources such as disputed seabed gas and oil deposits over large areas. The circumstances are difficult to predict in advance, of course. But the nature of such a violation would be so severe as to make it doubtful that automatic global sanctions could suffice as a response—at least, not across all plausible cases of breakout.[23]

It is worth underscoring what has been implicit in this discussion: many plausible violations of a nuclear disarmament treaty would be hard to prove. Even the existence of on-site inspection procedures would not guarantee resolution of murky cases, because the country suspected of having an illicit program might find an excuse to deny or delay access for inspectors. The situation would then be akin to Saddam Hussein's post-1991 Iraq. How should the international community respond if inspectors are denied access to suspected illicit weapons sites? What of highly suspicious microbiological research activity that involves the secret organization of dozens of top scientists in a hidden location but no smoking gun of illicit pathogens? What of fresh blueprints for a nuclear bomb discovered by inspectors—who are unable to find more concrete evidence of a bomb program? What of a major conventional military buildup that appears egregious to all concerned, yet is justified by the perpetrator not as preparation for an attack but as a defensive measure in the face of purportedly hostile neighbors?

These kinds of likely uncertainties are yet another complicating aspect of the future world one might envision under a nuclear disarmament regime. It will not be a simple world in which only the blatant and presumably unlikely development of nuclear weapons by a violator leads other countries to consider their options. It will be a world in which some type of major challenge to the nuclear disarmament regime might arise every so often—perhaps every decade or two, for example. Again, the regime should be understood as one of dismantlement, not necessarily permanent abolition, and it should be expected in advance that temporary reconstitution could well prove necessary at some point.

Beyond these legal and treaty matters, what types of physical preparations should be made to help with reconstitution, should it someday be necessary? Again, the goal would be largely, if not principally, to deter treaty violations by making sure any would-be cheater knew that its actions would not catch the rest of the international community unaware and would not go unanswered.

To repeat, bomb-ready fissile materials should not be retained. When writing about nuclear disarmament in the early 1980s, Jonathan Schell proposed dismantling weapons but keeping a stock of fissile material ready just in case—deterrence without weapons.[24] This idea goes a step beyond Bruce Blair's well-known and persuasive campaign, joined by many others over the years, for de-alerting nuclear forces.[25] But neither de-alerted nuclear weapons nor bomb-ready fissile materials should be retained under a nuclear disarmament regime. A world without nuclear weapons but full of fissile materials only steps away from being assembled into bombs would seem oxymoronic—and perhaps not worth the trouble to build. Fissile materials are also the most difficult components of nuclear weapons to develop or create, of course, so a nuclear disarmament regime designed to be verifiable and to give adequate warning of any violations should not allow their existence. Stockpiles of fissile materials, at least as much as advanced, assembled bombs mated to delivery vehicles, represent the world's greatest collective worry and collective threat in the age of terrorism. They are hard to make, easy to hide, dangerous if lost, and not particularly difficult to fashion into weapons. There is no reason they need to exist on the planet under a nuclear disarmament regime, even for purposes of retaining a latent reconstitution capability.

It does make sense, however, to preserve other latent capabilities for reconstitution. These include lists of people—the kinds of scientists and technicians who would be needed in a bomb program. Other items to track include hardware, materials, and infrastructure—uranium enrichment facilities, sophisticated machine shops where bombs might be built, laboratories for making conventional explosives. Such reconstitution plans should include substantial amounts of redundancy as a hedge against sabotage or preemptive attack.

Getting rid of the weapons and fissile materials but keeping "warm" the lists of people who can regenerate them as well as the facilities needed to do so strikes the right balance in a nuclear disarmament regime. Eliminating weapons, some weapons delivery vehicles, fissile materials, plutonium reprocessing capabilities, these steps are verifiable—if not perfectly, at least to a degree. Erasing the knowledge of how to make the bomb, along with the understanding of nuclear physics among a country's technical classes, is neither feasible nor verifiable. Moreover, confirming that another country has no secret list of scientists, technologies, and facilities that would be needed to rebuild a nuclear arsenal would also be impractical. There is thus no reason to try to ban such lists and plans; it is too hard to do.[26] And there is no reason for the United States to abstain from maintaining such lists itself, as a hedge against unforeseen developments; in fact, the United States should do so. With this approach, it could rebuild some nuclear inventory within a number of months.

That is a good time frame for purposes of a nuclear disarmament treaty. If states could rebuild arsenals in just weeks, there would be little time to deliberate if suspected violations were uncovered, and the world would always be on the verge of rearming fast. If, however, years were required to rebuild nuclear arms, a great deal of havoc could be caused in the meantime by an aggressive state, depending on the scenario. The offending state might invade a neighbor with conventional forces and threaten to use secretly rebuilt nuclear forces against any state coming to the victim's aid, for example. In that event, a country like the United States might be deterred so long that the conquest of the victim state might begin to seem like a fait accompli. The American people might lose heart and choose not to support an extended period of rebuilding a nuclear arsenal while also preparing conventional forces for a possible counterinvasion. But if rearmament could be accomplished over a period of months, as would surely be the case for any world with significant ongoing use of nuclear power, the type of resolve that the United States maintained after the Iraqi invasion of Kuwait in August of 1990 until Operation Desert Storm was launched the following January, or in the one to two years after September 11, 2001, could likely be generated and sustained.

Would the United States and other countries really be able to afford a several-month delay in response to an aggression? In theory, the answer might not be so obvious. Certainly a Soviet-scale nuclear arsenal in the hands of an aggressor could be used to threaten all known concentrations of nuclear physics research, and of nuclear physicists, in the country—potentially preventing the United States from rebuilding its nuclear deterrent. But this would require lots of bombs, given the number of major physics research facilities, locations of fissile material concentrations, and machining facilities in the country—today the list would include half a dozen Department of Energy laboratories, about 100 nuclear reactors, at least several dozen major metals processing centers, and another several dozen major university physics laboratories.[27] Several dozen airfields hosting major commercial and civilian aircraft would also likely have to be targeted to eliminate top candidates for delivery vehicles of any weapons used for retaliation. To make retaliation impractical in short order, therefore, at a bare minimum several hundred sites would need to be destroyed or severely damaged. Even if in theory a cold war–vintage Soviet (or American) arsenal might have been up to the task on paper, a country breaking out from a nuclear disarmament regime and needing to make hundreds of strikes from a standing start would be extremely hard pressed to attempt it given the constraints imposed by the regime's verification system. (It is worth noting that fewer warheads could pose a mortal threat to a smaller state such as Israel.[28] Thus, in a nuclear disarmament regime, the U.S. obligation to deter nuclear threats or attacks against other countries would grow in some ways. Such countries could be expected to give up or forgo their own arsenals only if they were confident that another country was helping ensure their security.)

Some have argued that, with time, nuclear expertise will atrophy so much that any country will find it very difficult to build or rebuild the bomb.[29] That seems incorrect. To be sure, fluency with the details of the bomb will be lost as those who have actually worked with nuclear devices retire in the decades to come. But the basics of nuclear physics are not so easy to forget. Rebuilding a large arsenal might be harder with the nuclear weapons novices of, say, the twenty-second century. But their command of nuclear physics, of precise machining methods, and of the basic understanding of what goes into any device creating a self-sustaining chain reaction is unlikely to be lost. That may mean that mankind has to live, for centuries to come, with the fact that scientists will be capable of building nuclear weapons fairly quickly if and when they have a national-scale effort to back them up. That may be sobering at one level, but it is also reassuring, for it means that if world events evolve in a direction that makes reconstitution seem desirable, rearming will in fact be feasible indefinitely into the future.

5   THE NEAR-TERM AGENDA

FOR THOSE WHO SUPPORT the nuclear disarmament vision but recognize the practical impediments to achieving it in the near future, the near-term nuclear agenda is unclear. Most advocates of global zero and other possible approaches to nuclear disarmament will naturally support a classic arms control agenda of further reductions in offensive forces, ratification of the Comprehensive Test Ban Treaty (CTBT), and the like. But is there any way in which the nuclear disarmament agenda meaningfully diverges from, or goes beyond, such traditional measures in the coming years?

Addressing this question with focus is important. Otherwise, the new effort to rid the world of nuclear weapons risks being cynical, meaningless, or counterproductive. It could be cynical if, after statements such as President Obama's Prague speech in April 2009, the great powers revert to classic behavior with no real hope or even intention of moving toward zero. It could be meaningless if they sincerely support the goal but do nothing beyond the next round of arms cuts to pursue it. After all, nuclear abolition has been an official goal of U.S. nuclear policy for forty years, to little apparent effect. Many arms control efforts have occurred subsequently, but they were motivated by desires to reduce forces, advance stability and transparency, save money, improve safety, and check proliferation—not to rid the world of this category of armament altogether. On the other hand, prudence is required. It is critically important not to support any and all bold ideas out of enthusiasm for disarmament, since doing so could worsen, rather than mitigate, the risks of proliferation. The trick is to be bold without being careless or naïve, to move forward assertively without rushing. The following agenda, several elements of which are developed in further detail below, would seem to fit the bill.

—The goal of nuclear disarmament should lead to deeper, quicker, and more permanent U.S. and Russian arms cuts than might otherwise be pursued in the aftermath of the New START Treaty, signed by Russia and the United States in April 2010.

—Steps to improve verification in new areas, such as warhead dismantlement and a cutoff of fissile material production, should be pursued faster than might otherwise be the case—largely to develop procedures that could be of use for a nuclear disarmament regime down the road.

—Highly enriched uranium (HEU) should be eliminated even more quickly than previously planned, for example, from U.S. aircraft carriers as well as from U.S., U.K., and Indian nuclear submarines. (Russia also uses fairly highly enriched uranium in submarines and icebreakers that could be replaced over time with less highly enriched uranium.)[1]

—Nuclear doctrine should move more clearly in the direction of minimizing the role of nuclear weapons in current security policy, while retaining the caveat about possible future "superbug" pathogens discussed in chapter 3. The Obama administration's 2010 Nuclear Posture Review is consistent with my recommendations on this point, although it retains more nuclear options against Iran and North Korea than seem optimal.

—Missile defenses would seek to create collaborative ventures as much as possible, recognizing that cooperation on defenses will be essential if the great powers are to move together toward zero.

(The great powers should also show restraint in using space for offensive military purposes, though as I have argued elsewhere, it is difficult to create effective and verifiable arms control in this arena. Most measures should therefore be informal, with the possible exception of a negotiated ban on explosions that would cause debris above a certain altitude in space.)[2]

Offensive Nuclear Weapons

Further deep nuclear force cuts are possible now. Given the huge cold war arsenals the superpowers built up, considerable fractions of which remain today, the United States and Russia can move further in the general direction of zero without jeopardizing the core elements of nuclear deterrence. Beyond the simple matter of numbers, there is ample opportunity to minimize the role of nuclear weapons in military doctrine and nuclear deterrence concepts and to reduce the alert levels of remaining arsenals.

From the viewpoint of a nuclear disarmament advocate, existing nuclear war–planning logic that is focused on creation of a single integrated operational plan is essentially irrelevant to force sizing. That does not mean that the only targets for weapons today should be cities. It does mean, however, that the notion of synchronized, carefully orchestrated attacks against a wide range of nuclear, conventional military, leadership, and possibly economic assets is anachronistic—if indeed it ever made sense. Having a portfolio of possible "aimpoints" to attack in the event that retaliation was ever necessary is wise. In that regard, some intelligence work would continue to be needed even in a denuclearized world to maintain a database on plausible targets in plausible aggressor countries should nuclear weapons ever need to be reconstituted. But the whole notion of a single integrated operational plan, with its emphasis on comprehensive and simultaneous effects against an enemy's target base, is simply unnecessary and indeed unsound strategically.

Of course, reaching that conclusion does not trivialize the remaining task of sizing and shaping nuclear forces. First, the above conclusion works best when the United States and Russia *both* agree with it; until they do, some residual effects from patterns of cold war thinking may be difficult to extirpate. Second, as noted, some flexibility in targeting and weapons delivery capability is still needed. Third, deep cuts must not get too far ahead of verification capabilities and are truly possible only when all nuclear weapons inventories and fissile material stocks are brought within the regime. Fourth, the possible effects on China of deep U.S. and Russian arms reductions must not be dismissed; it would be regrettable on multiple fronts if in their haste to pursue nuclear disarmament, Washington and Moscow encouraged a buildup by Beijing.

Putting these concerns together, if it could be negotiated and properly implemented and verified, a treaty that would limit each nuclear superpower to 1,000 total warheads makes sense in the near term. Reaching agreement on that number would be a dramatic achievement. The 2010 New START Treaty that would cut Russian and American inventories to 1,550 deployed strategic warheads each and total deployed strategic delivery vehicles to 700 each is far less ambitious.[3] While worthwhile, these cuts reflect arms control incrementalism—an additional reduction of about 10 percent beyond what Presidents George W. Bush and Vladimir Putin had negotiated under the 2002 Moscow Treaty. That Moscow accord, also known as the Strategic Offensive Reduction Treaty (or SORT), required that deployed offensive forces total no more than 1,700 to 2,200 warheads by 2012.[4]

To be sure, the 2010 accord has great value as a way of "resetting" U.S.-Russian relations, restoring greater rigor to arms control verification and implementation, and limiting buildup capacity through tighter caps on delivery vehicles. But it is not otherwise very dramatic. Nor would the next likely treaty be dramatic; even if it aimed for around 1,200 strategic warheads on a side, with some caps on excess inventories, as seems likely as of this writing, the reductions would remain on the same glide path as before. Again, additional reductions would be in the range of 10 to 20 percent. This is the sort of thing one might expect from a business-as-usual approach, not from one informed by a nuclear zero ambition.

Focusing on a treaty to reduce to 1,000 total warheads on a side, not only signed but also fully implemented by 2020, would allow each superpower to argue accurately that it had cut nuclear inventories by 95 percent relative to cold war highs and by roughly 90 percent compared with weapons inventories of 2010. Such a treaty would require a seriousness about tactical and reserve warhead inventories because they would have to be slashed a great deal under any conceivable implementation plan. Proposing such a reduction would demonstrably go beyond the kinds of nuclear posture reviews that tend to emerge from the Department of Defense—which remains relatively conservative on nuclear force planning—and signify a much more White House–driven process than has been the norm in the U.S. context. Similar breakthroughs in approach and in overcoming domestic political constraints would be needed in Russia, too.[5]

Paring back to 1,000 total warheads on a side would be ambitious but not reckless. If most remaining warheads were on strategic launchers, as would be likely, the strategic reduction would amount to less than 50 percent relative to New START levels. Many targeting options beyond countercity strikes would be preserved. For example, major military and industrial powers tend to have roughly dozens (as opposed to hundreds or thousands) of each of the following types of major assets: major metals production facilities, major oil refineries, large airfields and military marshaling yards, central military supply depots, large ports, and strategic command and control facilities.[6] It does not seem credible that these would all be attacked under any plausible scenario;

thoughtful students of nuclear weapons have found the notion of even a few weapons ever being used so cataclysmic as to transcend the specific military effects of the weapons used. But thinking in these terms does show that meaningful targeting options would remain even with much smaller arsenals and with a nuclear planning paradigm that no longer viewed adversarial nuclear forces as the central focus of its war plans. A reduction to around 1,000 warheads each would keep U.S. and Russian force levels far above those of other states—and far above and beyond what any serious war-fighting operation could ever employ.

Other powers need not be part of this treaty. However, it would be highly desirable and perhaps necessary that they at least make politically binding commitments to cap their existing arsenals at roughly current sizes. Informal, unilateral, reciprocated steps have been helpful in arms control before (such as those taken by the United States and Soviet Union as the cold war was ending), and such measures could be helpful here too.[7] Given that countries such as China and India have historically prided themselves on their relative nuclear restraint, such caps may well prove feasible.[8]

As noted, the proposed treaty would cover all U.S. and Russian nuclear warheads.[9] However, Russia might not be enthusiastic about such a sweeping accord. In that event, an initial strategic accord focused on 2020 could constrain the two countries to 1,000 deployed strategic warheads each. Limits on tactical and surplus warheads could be treated separately, and perhaps incrementally, over the coming decade rather than being combined with strategic limits. This approach would lack the clarity and symbolism of a comprehensive 1,000 warhead accord but might, over time, leave the two countries in a similar place.[10]

My proposal for a U.S. nuclear force posture under a 1,000 warhead accord preserves the so-called triad, including land-based missiles and bombers. Some advocate greater, if not complete, reliance on the submarine force after any such deep cuts. Submarines are survivable only when at sea, however, and keeping them at sea with their warheads aboard runs counter to the vision of "de-alerting" nuclear forces so that they are not on a hair trigger as they were during the cold war. At some point warheads may no longer be deployed on missiles, in the interest of greater safety, and force structure decisions should be made accordingly. It may be possible to store warheads in some of the tubes currently used for missiles, de-mated from submarine-launched ballistic missiles (SLBMs), as a de-alerting concept, an idea worthy of further examination.[11] But for the foreseeable future, maintaining a triad rather than relying just on submarines or another single type of system still makes sense. So my recommended alternative force posture would feature a mix.

—Six Trident submarines, each with 100 warheads aboard, down from fourteen submarines today, and quite likely twelve to fourteen under the New START Treaty. (Each submarine is armed with twenty-four Trident II or D5 missiles, carrying a grand total of somewhat more than 1,000 warheads among them as of 2010. Nine submarines normally focus on the Pacific and five on the Atlantic). The six would operate as they do today, out of one port on the East Coast and one on the West Coast. Two submarines could be at sea at a time to preserve the arsenal's survivability.[12]

—100 land-based, single-warhead Minuteman III missiles in hardened silos in the Midwest (down from 450 today, with a total of about 550 deployed warheads). A certain number of conventionally armed missiles might be exempted from caps, up to a maximum number of perhaps several dozen, if that proved negotiable.[13]

—300 warheads deliverable by B-52 or B-2 bomber (down from about 500 in 2009), with three to four bases in the United States equipped to handle the warheads and thirty planes capable of delivering them. Currently twenty B-2 bombers and fifty-six B-52 bombers are dedicated to the nuclear mission, each capable of carrying 16 to 20 warheads.[14]

The savings from this force posture over the next decade would be principally in areas of operations and support, since plans for modernizing the offensive nuclear force are modest. The military is currently maintaining and, when necessary, refurbishing Minuteman missiles and Trident submarine-based capabilities and is not currently developing replacement systems. Some longer-term programs would eventually be scaled back under a smaller force posture. But the main near-term savings would arise from reductions in the number of intercontinental ballistic missiles (ICBMs) (up to 350 missiles) and submarines (up to eight vessels), as well as by stopping production of D5 missiles a few years earlier than now planned (the program is currently scheduled to go through 2013). The ICBMs each cost about $2.5 million a year to operate, the submarines about $70 million each, making for total savings of about $1.5 billion a year if this option can be implemented.[15] No savings are assumed for the bomber fleet, given its dual-purpose roles; conventional missions would give reason to sustain the force structure even in light of nuclear cutbacks.

As noted, this U.S.-Russian treaty should be accompanied, at a minimum, by statements from the medium-size nuclear powers promising restraint in the future growth and modernization of their militaries. China in particular needs to commit to a cap near its current levels. To be sure, China's overall history with nuclear forces is one of restraint, and its current modernization program is limited in scope. But some Chinese military analysts and officials have indicated not only that they support a Chinese buildup but also that they expect the two nuclear superpowers to take major, unreciprocated steps; some even express opposition to nuclear disarmament because it could strengthen the United States in light of its conventional military superiority.[16] This combination of attitudes is potentially problematic. While China need not take major steps now, it is important that Beijing not exploit the current push toward lower U.S. and Russian numbers by trying to catch up with these countries.

In near-term nuclear doctrine decisions, the United States should also clarify that the circumstances are extremely rare under which it would ever use nuclear weapons for any purpose other than deterring nuclear use by others. Historically, as noted earlier, the United States has maintained ambiguity on this point, avoiding a nuclear no-first-use policy. This was true in the cold war— when large Warsaw Pact armies made Western leaders feel the need for a nuclear deterrent against possible conventional aggression. It remained true when the George W. Bush administration expanded the possible role of nuclear weapons in the post-9/11 world.[17] It was true in between as well. The administration of George H. W. Bush maintained a broad range of possible purposes for nuclear weapons even after the collapse of the Warsaw Pact as well as the Soviet Union itself. In 1992, for example, its national military strategy mentioned the possible role of nuclear weapons "as a hedge against the emergence of an overwhelming conventional threat" should one again present itself. The strategy document also spoke of deterring an enemy's use of weapons of mass destruction in general, not just nuclear weapons specifically, as a role for American nuclear forces.[18] The Clinton administration maintained ambiguity on the matter as well. Most of its policy documents kept to a narrow rhetorical role for nuclear weapons, emphasizing that American nuclear capabilities were designed to deter the use of nuclear weapons by others.[19] However, the Clinton administration did not go along with the proposal of some NATO countries such as Germany and Canada to consider a no-first-use doctrine; it ultimately preserved flexibility on the matter.[20]

As argued in chapter 3, it is not logical to allow an enemy to threaten or use an advanced biological pathogen against the United States or its allies without fear of an American nuclear response. Biological weapons are potentially every bit as devastating, indiscriminate, and lethal as nuclear weapons. At some future point, Washington may find it necessary to remind possible adversaries that a decision on their part to develop and deploy— or, heaven forbid, use—an advanced pathogen that was highly contagious, highly lethal, and very difficult to inoculate against or treat could lead to an American nuclear response.

But that day is not near. The United States therefore can and should be more willing to circumscribe the conditions under which it might use nuclear weapons. As a matter of state policy today, the United States should declare that it would *not* use nuclear weapons against contemporary chemical and biological arms that enemies might use against America. The Obama administration's 2010 Nuclear Posture Review moved in the right direction in this regard. However, it unnecessarily preserved nuclear exemptions for dealing with North Korea and Iran in the near future, even if those states do not use nuclear weapons in any attack themselves.

The goal of eliminating nuclear weapons also provides added impetus to take today's weapons off ready-fire alert. This approach has been suggested by scholars such as Bruce Blair for many years, as well as by the Canberra Commission on the Elimination of Nuclear Weapons in 1996.[21] A logical near-term step might be to take all warheads off silo-based ICBMs. The Obama administration, however, did not countenance any such step, or other lowering of ICBM alert status, in its 2010 Nuclear Posture Review (although it continued the policy of normally targeting ICBMs and SLBMs into open ocean spaces as an additional safety measure).[22] De-alerting would not leave the missiles themselves any more vulnerable than they are today. With time, pulling warheads off SLBMs would be worthy of consideration as well, but that would require a much more complete rethinking of the notion of warhead survivability. Other countries that rely on their nuclear deterrents already have lower-alert practices than do the United States and Russia, however, so some de-alerting would not appear to constitute a setback to U.S. security or a weakening of the credibility of the U.S. deterrent.[23]

The United States, after consultation with allies and in parallel with Russian changes, can also take steps to lower nuclear capabilities in forward areas. It no longer has any military need for nuclear weapons in Europe or for tactical fighter jets that can carry nuclear weapons.[24] These can be bargaining chips in future arms control negotiations.

The Comprehensive Test Ban Treaty

Ratification of the Comprehensive Test Ban Treaty and its entry into force have been explicitly identified by many nonnuclear weapons states as their top arms control priority in recent years. More specifically, the CTBT, negotiated in the 1990s and intended to ban all nuclear tests of any kind, is what they demand of the established nuclear powers as a condition for their continued willingness to forgo nuclear weapons themselves—while also agreeing to place their civilian nuclear programs under the additional protocol of the International Atomic Energy Agency, or IAEA (which provides for inspections of facilities). The Nuclear Non-Proliferation Treaty (NPT) was extended indefinitely in 1995 "largely because the long-stalled comprehensive test ban . . . seemed at last certain of adoption," according to the man who presided over the decisionmaking process.[25] The CTBT is thus directly linked to what many consider the top national security priority of the United States—stopping nuclear proliferation.

President George W. Bush did not favor the CTBT. But with his presidency completed, treaty advocates can be relieved that he did nothing that irreversibly sank its prospects. President Bush did not "unsign" the treaty, as he was once purported to have considered doing; he also did not test nuclear weapons during his tenure in office. His administration periodically sought funds to research new types of nuclear warheads that would have likely required testing somewhere down the road, but Congress severely constrained these research efforts.

Whatever harm done to the nuclear nonproliferation regime during the Bush years, with the North Korean nuclear breakout in 2003 and its test in 2006 leading the way, was probably not primarily the result of U.S. policy on nuclear testing. Even during the pro-CTBT Clinton administration, India and Pakistan became de facto nuclear powers, complete with testing, so the damage done to the global taboo on nuclear testing during the Bush years is roughly comparable to that of the 1990s. That said, recalling the history of the 1990s, when North Korea also is believed to have begun (or attempted to begin) an underground uranium enrichment operation and when Iran continued work on its nuclear agenda as well, is sobering because it reminds those who would forget that having a pro–arms control American president hardly guarantees headway on the nonproliferation agenda. (Then again, an administration skeptical of arms control does not guarantee progress either, of course, as the recent North Korea experience under President George W. Bush strongly suggests.)

President Obama can and should push for ratification and implementation of the CTBT, a goal of nuclear arms control and nonproliferation advocates for half a century now. Among existing nuclear weapons states, France, the United Kingdom, and Russia have already ratified the treaty.[26] China has pledged to follow suit if the United States ratifies, and some favorable indications have been expressed at times by Israel and India as well, although it is not yet clear what India would do.[27]

Yet huge challenges must be addressed before the CTBT can be implemented. At the U.S. domestic political level, the challenge will be ratification. The Republican caucus voted almost unanimously against the CTBT in 1999 (the Bush administration never resubmitted it for ratification); opposition was hardly limited to the most conservative members. Many avowed internationalists, who have supported other treaties in the past and who value a U.S. foreign policy that promotes multilateralism and the pursuit of international consensus on key issues, opposed the CTBT. Former Republican secretaries of state George Shultz and Henry Kissinger are among those now favoring ratification, but many Republican senators are on record in opposition.[28] They have raised questions that will have to be answered if a future CTBT ratification vote is to gain the support of ten to fifteen or more Republican senators—the minimum that likely will be needed not only to ensure passage, which requires a two-thirds majority, but to establish strong bipartisan support for continuing the policy in the future.

The key questions about the CTBT are these. Can such a treaty be verified? Does it really help enhance the nonproliferation agenda and, if so, how? Does it allow the United States to ensure the long-term reliability of its existing arsenal in a manner that provides robust deterrence for itself and its allies? Finally, to the extent that might be judged necessary, is the treaty consistent with future U.S. nuclear weapons needs? The case that verifiability and stockpile reliability can both be ensured under a CTBT has strengthened over the past ten years.[29] But these subjects still require serious discussion, and each is considered below.

In pursuing CTBT ratification, advocates will have to be extremely careful in dealing with the question of pursuing complete nuclear disarmament. Were advocates of the CTBT to be seen as *assuming* adoption of a nuclear disarmament accord within a certain time frame as part of their argument for treaty ratification, the treaty's prospects could be set back. Many, if not most, CTBT skeptics in the United States are worried that the treaty would weaken the U.S. nuclear deterrent; they view this possibility as a major liability of the treaty, given the state of international politics today, and not an advantage for its indirect contribution to the nuclear disarmament cause.[30] Indeed, if the CTBT were to weaken the United States' nuclear deterrent in the short term, it *would* be a bad idea. The world is not ready for nuclear disarmament—and more to the point, no one can predict when it will be. CTBT skeptics must thus be reassured about the arsenal's robustness for the foreseeable future if ratification is to have any chance. CTBT advocates should not imply that a vote for the testing ban is tantamount to a vote for nuclear zero.

But for nuclear disarmament proponents, the CTBT is in fact very important. U.S. ratification of the CTBT as soon as possible is a top priority for them. If ratification fails, one can soldier on with offensive arms cuts and perhaps a fissile material cutoff treaty. But failure to ratify the CTBT could weaken support for the NPT regime from nonnuclear states that have increasingly attempted to link the two accords, and new momentum toward a 1,000 warhead regime would become more difficult to mobilize in the United States too. More generally, disarmament advocates will find it harder to sustain their hope that the Obama presidency can help jumpstart more serious changes in the way the international community views nuclear weapons.

Some have suggested that a reason to preserve U.S. options for future nuclear testing relates to the potential need for new types of warheads to accomplish new missions. The idea of developing a nuclear weapon that could burrow underground *before* detonating has recently gained some appeal—not least because countries such as North Korea and Iran are responding to the United States' increasingly precise conventional weaponry by hiding key weapons programs well below the planet's surface. One possible argument for such a warhead is to increase its overall destructive depth. In theory, the United States could modify the largest nuclear weapons in its stockpile to penetrate the earth. This approach would roughly double the destructive reach of the most powerful weapons in the current arsenal, according to physicist Michael Levi. But if an enemy can avoid weapons in the current arsenal, it could avoid the more powerful bombs by digging deeper underground. Given the quality of modern drilling equipment, that is not an onerous task. Nor would the use of ground-penetrating weapons prevent radioactive fallout. Given limits on the hardness of materials and other basic physics, no useful nuclear weapon could penetrate the earth far enough to keep the radioactive effects of its blast entirely below ground.

Such weapons could indeed reduce fallout. As a rule of thumb, the explosive yield of a weapon converted into an earth penetrator can be reduced tenfold (or more) while the weapon would have the same destructive capability against underground targets as a normal weapon would have.[31] That would reduce fallout by a factor of ten as well—a meaningful change. But is it really enough to change the basic usability of a nuclear device? Such a weapon would still produce a huge amount of fallout. Its use would still break the nuclear taboo. It would still be capable of destroying underground targets only if their locations were precisely known, in which case conventional weapons or special forces might be able to neutralize the site.

CTBT Verification

What of verification for the CTBT? In fact, large nuclear weapons detonations are relatively easy to detect. If they are in the atmosphere (in violation of the atmospheric test ban treaty), they are usually visible from satellite and identifiable by their characteristic radiation distribution. Because such tests are so hard to hide reliably, no country trying to keep its nuclear capabilities secret has tested in the atmosphere in recent decades. (South Africa and Israel might have done so but were effectively caught in the process in 1979, before the former made the impressive decision under President F. W. de Klerk in 1990 to end its nuclear weapons program and verifiably destroy its existing arsenal of six weapons and components for a seventh. South Africa subsequently relinquished its nuclear materials to international authorities and joined the NPT.[32])

Underground detonations, which are more common, can be detected through seismic monitoring, provided they reach a certain size. Any weapon of kiloton power or above (the Hiroshima and Nagasaki bombs were in the ten to twenty kiloton range) can be "heard" in this way. In other words, any weapon with significant military potential tested at its full strength is very likely to be noticed. U.S. seismic arrays are found throughout much of Eurasia's periphery, for example, and even tests elsewhere could generally be picked up.

Even though it either "fizzled" or was designed to have a small yield in the first place (under one kiloton), the North Korean test in October 2006 was detected and clearly identified as a nuclear burst.[33] Detection of that test gives added confidence that even "decoupled" tests carried out in large artificial underground caverns created specifically for that purpose could be detected if their power were of militarily significant magnitude.[34] Monitoring sensitivity is improving worldwide as the International Monitoring System is further expanded to include 321 monitoring stations in ninety countries. Of these, 80 will use air sampling to look for radionuclides released by possible nuclear explosions, 60 will monitor the atmosphere for low-frequency sound waves characteristic of nuclear bursts, 11 will be underwater acoustic stations, and 50 will be primary seismic monitoring stations on land with another 120 acting in a supplementary mode.[35] Indeed, it may be possible to detect tests less than one-tenth the power of the North Korean explosion.[36] Twenty of the stations in the incomplete network operating in 2006 detected North Korea's explosion that year; 61 seismic stations noted the larger underground test North Korea conducted in 2009.[37]

There are only two viable ways to escape detection. First, test a device well below its intended military yield, through some type of modification of the weapon's physics. (The modification may, however, make the device so different from the actual class of weapon it is designed to represent that sophisticated extrapolation of the test results would be needed to deduce how the actual weapon would behave.) A country very sophisticated in nuclear technology might be able to conduct a test of a modified device that escaped international detection. But such engineering feats, difficult even for advanced nuclear powers, are most likely beyond the means of a fledgling nuclear power.

Second, as noted, dig out a very large underground cavity into which a weapon can be placed, thereby "decoupling" the blast from direct contact with the ground and allowing it to weaken before it reaches surrounding soil or rock and causes the earth to shake. This latter approach is arduous. And it does not make a weapon totally undetectable but simply changes the threshold yield at which it can be heard by U.S., Russian, and international seismic sensors.[38]

Nuclear verification capabilities have picked up the Indian, Pakistani, and North Korean nuclear tests—even the small, relatively unsuccessful ones—in the past dozen years and would be able to do so with high confidence for tests from those or other countries in the future. Verification capabilities are not airtight or perfect, but on balance these limitations are hardly grounds to oppose a test ban treaty.

Critics of the CTBT sometimes argue that an end to U.S. nuclear testing would not stop proliferation—or testing by others. Surely Kim Jong Il of North Korea, or Mahmoud Ahmadinejad of Iran, or even the leaders of Pakistan and India are relatively unimpressed by any U.S. nuclear restraint. The first two tyrants are not easily inspired by acts of moral courage by other states. India and Pakistan, for their part, tend to argue that a country like the United States with thousands of nuclear warheads in its inventory and almost 1,000 total nuclear tests under its belt is hardly in a position to deny others their nuclear rights (even as many Indians in particular continue to argue for a nuclear-free world and project regret that their own country ultimately felt the need to acquire nuclear weapons because of the actions of other powers[39]). Any of these states, so goes realist logic, will make nuclear-related decisions based much more on their own security environments and agendas than out of concern about a global movement to limit the bomb's spread and to lower its profile.

These are serious objections. But while regional security conditions do matter more than global arguments for most countries contemplating the bomb, a strong international message against proliferation can still affect their calculations. If there is a sense that "everyone is doing it," leaders teetering on the edge of going nuclear will feel less restraint about doing so—and perhaps even an obligation to protect their own countries from the potential nuclear weapons of their neighbors. In this regard, maintaining a strong international dissuasive force against nuclearization is important, for it affects perceptions of the likelihood of proliferation. Indeed, efforts to delegitimize the bomb over the past half century and those to reduce testing and reduce arsenals over the last four decades have helped convince governments in Argentina, Brazil, Chile, Egypt, Germany, Japan, Saudi Arabia, South Korea, and Taiwan not to pursue these weapons. Sometimes CTBT critics trivialize these accomplishments, noting, for example, that it would not be so bad if a country like Japan or Brazil got the bomb. But such arguments, even if partly right, ignore the fact that once one crosses the "nuclear tipping point" and momentum grows for getting the bomb, it will not be just the Japans and Brazils from this list that go nuclear.[40]

A CTBT would not physically prevent extremist states from getting the bomb, nor would it likely impress them with its moral force. But it would help reaffirm a norm, already acknowledged to a degree, that nuclear testing is unacceptable. That in turn would help discourage countries from testing the bomb for fear they will be punished if they do so. And if they test anyway, they will pay a price for it, which may persuade them (or others) not to repeat the mistake and not to continue further down the same path.

Admittedly, this logic did not apply very well to the cases of India and Pakistan, which have hardly suffered serious and lasting reprisal from the world community as a result of their testing. As a generally stable and peaceful democracy, India's transgression was not viewed as anxiously as North Korea's by the international community, and its nuclear buildup subsequently, while hardly inconsequential in scale, has been somewhat restrained.[41]

Pakistan's transgression did raise major worries, but America's need to work with Islamabad in the struggle against extremists soon trumped the nonproliferation imperative. However, the world reaction to North Korea's October 2006 test, including passage of a UN Security Council resolution limiting some types of world trade with North Korea, as well as the stronger measures adopted after its 2009 test, show that this argument has some meaning. Norms do matter because they help in pressuring violators. Until North Korea's tests, China and South Korea had largely protected Pyongyang from severe sanctions, even after it broke out of the NPT in 2003. But when North Korea went so far as to test a bomb, Beijing, Seoul, and Moscow all told Pyongyang it had gone too far and agreed to international economic reprisals against it.[42] It is also worth noting that Iran, for all of its efforts to develop nuclear technology, has shown some restraint to date and tried to dress up its activities under the guise of peaceful nuclear activities. Testing is inconsistent with such pretenses, which means that Iran will likely think twice about testing even if it someday produces enough fissile material to be able to do so. Or perhaps it will test just once, rather than five or ten times, making any resulting arsenal less reliable and quite possibly less sophisticated than it would otherwise be. Ratification of the CTBT would solidify this very worthwhile and helpful international opprobrium associated with nuclear testing.

As far as is known, every country trying to validate a nuclear capability has succeeded on the first try. Simple fission bombs are relatively complicated devices but generally not beyond the capacity of a country capable of enriching uranium or producing and reprocessing plutonium. However, developing advanced weapons—thermonuclear devices, devices capable of being delivered by missile, warheads capable of surviving atmospheric reentry and still performing correctly—is hard. Several countries including the United States have had difficulties, needing multiple tests and corrective procedures before establishing confidence with a given warhead design. Making it hard for proliferators to test will, therefore, among other benefits, make it harder for them to develop missile-mounted warheads of the type that would generally be most threatening against the United States and its allies.

Stockpile Reliability

What about the stockpile reliability issue? Again, as argued earlier, nuclear disarmament proponents must be careful not to let their support for banning the bomb cloud their judgment about the importance of the reliability question. Most political leaders and scholars agree that the United States needs a nuclear deterrent well into the foreseeable future. Since no one knows when or if nuclear disarmament will be attainable, the United States must do what is needed to keep its nuclear deterrent dependable.

Common sense would seem to support the position that, at some point in the future, testing will be needed to ensure the arsenal's reliability. How can one go ten or twenty or fifty or one hundred years without a single test and still be confident that the country's nuclear weapons will work? Equally important, how can one be sure that other countries will be deterred by a U.S. stockpile that at some point will be certified only by the experiments and tests of a generation of physicists long since retired or dead?

To be sure, the reliability of a given warhead class may decline as its components age. In a worst case, one category of warheads might become flawed without our knowing it; indeed, that has happened in the past. But through a combination of monitoring, testing, and remanufacturing of the individual components, conducting sophisticated experiments (short of actual nuclear detonations) on integrated devices, and perhaps introducing a new warhead type or two of extremely conservative design into the inventory to complement existing types, the overall dependability of the U.S. nuclear deterrent can remain very high. In other words, the arsenal might experience a slight reduction in its overall technical capacities, but its ability to exact a devastating response against anyone attacking the United States or its allies with weapons of mass destruction would still be unquestionable.

The Department of Energy has devoted huge sums of money to its stockpile stewardship program in an effort to understand as well as possible what happens within aging warheads and to predict the performance of those warheads once modified with slightly different materials in the future. It is a good program, and many experts now believe it will ensure the reliability of existing warheads for more than half a century. Indeed, recent independent studies, including those by the so-called JASON group, have suggested that plutonium pits in warheads—previously believed to be the most likely to degrade with time—will last for close to a century without major rebuilding.[43]

One element of this stockpile stewardship approach still gives some unease—its reliance on scientific theory and computation. For example, a key part of the effort uses elegant three-dimensional computer models based on computational physics to predict what will happen inside a warhead modified to use a new type (or amount) of chemical explosive. Other methods such as the so-called JASPER program and Z Machine are proving useful too, giving a clearer picture of what happens inside the physics package of a nuclear weapon. This type of science-based method is very good and worth sustaining vigorously, and it probably eliminates any immediate pressure to build new nuclear weapons.[44] But many wonder whether the United States can rely entirely on computations, simulations, and theory to ensure the nation's nuclear deterrent—and its security.

Thus, a final way to ensure confidence in the arsenal is worth keeping in mind—the development of a different, simpler kind of warhead to add to the arsenal as a form of insurance—not as a substitute for all existing warhead types, but as an addition to the portfolio. This warhead may not be needed anytime soon. But it could be a hedge against problems with the arsenal down the road. It is also a way to think about the challenge of nuclear arsenal reconstitution, should that somehow be needed in the future even after a nuclear disarmament accord is in effect.

Some would call this warhead a new design and question whether it was therefore consistent with President Obama's Nuclear Posture Review, which rules out new designs. But such a reliable warhead would not be new, in the sense that it would not push any technology barriers or seek to improve destructive performance. In addition, it would be largely an amalgam of concepts already seen in previous designs, not a creation of new ones. This approach would seek to use a conservative warhead design that allowed for slight errors in warhead performance and still ensured a robust nuclear yield.

Taking this approach might lead to a somewhat heavier warhead (meaning the number that could be carried on a given missile or bomber would have to be reduced), or a lower-yield warhead (meaning that a hardened Russian missile silo might not be so easily destroyed, for example). But for most purposes of deterrence, this approach is generally sound—weapons designers tend to agree that very reliable warheads can be produced if performance criteria are relaxed. It would also lead to less use of extremely toxic materials such as beryllium, and to safer types of conventional explosives that are less prone to accidental detonation, than is the case for some warheads in the current arsenal.[45] Indeed, in the extremely unlikely event that a nuclear weapon needed to be used, having a smaller-yield weapon available would be preferable because it would be less destructive. (Today's warheads themselves can provide lower yields in certain ranges by removal of the warhead secondary, the part of the bomb that produces the main fusion effect and thus most of its overall power.)[46] Some would oppose such changes on the ground that they could lower the threshold against nuclear use because fewer people would be killed by an explosion. The benefit of the lives saved from a smaller weapon would outweigh any slight increase in the risk of it being used carelessly, however; no sane policymaker would cross the nuclear taboo lightly just because a future weapon might have only twice the Hiroshima bomb yield rather than ten times that yield. There is not a major case for smaller bombs today, but they would not be dangerous to possess either.

The Bush administration and Congress both showed interest in a "reliable replacement warhead" (RRW) concept. Defense Secretary Robert Gates once effectively viewed it as a precondition for U.S. ratification of the CTBT.[47] It was only a research concept, and a controversial one at that, with Congress not always willing to provide funding even for research.[48] But while the RRW was controversial, both at home and abroad, the idea of building a conservative warhead design—based principally on old concepts, not new ones—makes sense on balance, at least as an option. Simple warhead designs are quite robust—recall that the Hiroshima bomb (a gun-assembly uranium device) was not even tested before being used. Over time, conservative designs could be added to the arsenal in modest numbers.

With a 1,000 warhead force not requiring testing, the United States could eliminate one of its three major weapons laboratories devoted largely to oversight of the nuclear arsenal. In addition, it need not construct a dedicated plutonium pit production facility; the modest capability at Los Alamos will suffice. Any building and deployment of a more conservative warhead design can happen gradually, in keeping with the limited capacities of the existing pit facility. These changes together would allow average annual savings of about $1 billion in the Energy Department's overall nuclear weapons budget.[49] About half of these savings would come from forgoing the new pit production facility, and the other half from gradually ending the nuclear weapons research at one of the three main laboratories.[50] The prospect of such savings could help produce new or stronger constituencies for nuclear weapons cutbacks in the coming years, when defense budgets, as well as federal budgets more generally, are expected to undergo significant belt-tightening measures in response to the nation's fiscal plight.

Warhead Dismantlement, HEU Use, and a Fissile Cutoff

A near-term agenda that could underpin a future nuclear disarmament treaty would take steps to improve verification in new areas such as warhead dismantlement, as well as a cutoff in the production of fissile materials. The agenda would also push for rapid reductions in the use of highly enriched uranium. As argued in chapter 3, verification that is good enough to make a nuclear elimination pact truly robust is unrealistic—not only now but indefinitely, probably forever. Because of the legacy of the cold war, the United States and its allies are unlikely ever to be fully confident that Russia has made its many stocks of fissile materials open to verification, or even fully accounted for them itself. As a result, a precondition to a nuclear disarmament accord is probably a strategic situation in which a Russian attack against the West becomes virtually as unthinkable as a French or British attack on the United States would be today. Beyond that, verification will need to become good enough to catch an extremist state bent on breaking out of a nuclear disarmament accord and threatening other states *before* it is in a position to wreak havoc. Verification must be able to ensure that a future rogue state such as today's Iran, North Korea, or Myanmar does not build a large enough arsenal—perhaps dozens of weapons—to have a strategically dominant capability long enough to be tempted to use it for purposes of blackmail.

Reaching such a threshold of verifiability requires attention principally to stockpiles of fissile materials and the technologies used to produce them. These are the most demanding prerequisites to any bomb program for a proliferant nation. The kinds of verification needed in the future are thus closer to the kinds of activities carried out by the IAEA today than through START or SORT accords. And it is in these areas that further progress is needed, before a nuclear disarmament accord can be seriously pursued.

Work in three specific areas will be key: a fissile material cut-off treaty, a warhead dismantlement verification concept, and a means of reducing existing stocks of fissile materials. The last of the three primarily concerns the United States and Russia. Although some considerable uncertainty will remain about the size of their inventories of plutonium and highly enriched uranium, reducing that uncertainty is required to show sincerity of purpose and to minimize the risks of illicit transfer of excess materials to a proliferating state in the future.

Consider these arms control efforts one by one. Serious negotiations on a fissile cutoff treaty are currently being blocked, primarily by Pakistan, at the Conference on Disarmament in Geneva.[51] That is an unsurprising consequence of the current state of security affairs in South Asia, and yet another indication of the importance of resolving major outstanding interstate conflicts before expecting that a nuclear disarmament pact could be attained. Were progress to become possible, it should be pursued. Any accord should cover as many facilities and materials as possible, to include those related to military as well as civilian purposes, including in current weapons states (indeed, they might not wait for such an accord, volunteering to have some facilities monitored sooner, as suggested by Scott Sagan and others).[52] Otherwise the treaty would have too many holes to be meaningful, and the nuclear superpowers in particular would fail to show sincerity of intention.[53] The verification protocols for such a treaty would need to continue strengthening monitoring capabilities across the board in anticipation of an ultimate nuclear disarmament accord, and ultimately cover all relevant sites in all states. En route to that goal, no backtracking should occur anywhere in any state. This implies retention of the so-called Additional Protocol of the International Atomic Energy Agency, which allows monitoring of all nuclear-related facilities and some investigation powers regarding suspected illicit activity, wherever it is currently in effect, and extension of the concept elsewhere.[54] It is also important to try to limit the number of states with full fuel-cycle technologies, notably those needed to enrich uranium or reprocess plutonium, to minimize the number of places where monitoring must be intense, and to make it harder for states with suspect motives to gain access to such technologies. Such efforts are already under way, even in the context of the current NPT and near-term nonproliferation agenda, and must be continued.[55] Limiting the number of sites where nuclear waste is stored would also be prudent.[56]

The near-term arms control agenda should also accelerate efforts to eliminate highly enriched uranium from nuclear submarines, research reactors, and other places where it is still used. Without such an effort, loopholes will remain in the fissile cutoff scheme. These loopholes might not be particularly worrying in regard to U.S.-Russian arms control in the short term (given the relatively modest amounts of material at issue), but they could sink a global nuclear disarmament accord.

Taking such measures in regard to superpower HEU would strengthen the hand of existing nuclear states as they seek to persuade other countries to move away from the use of HEU in various research reactors and similar facilities. Such efforts are under way already but have a long way to go. President Obama laid out an accelerated plan for securing all vulnerable nuclear material of a bomb-ready nature within four years at his April 5, 2009, Prague speech on nuclear disarmament and followed up usefully at the April 2010 Washington Nuclear Security Summit.[57]

An effective nuclear disarmament accord is also hard to imagine while plutonium is still being reprocessed widely for use in reactors. With reprocessing, bomb-ready fissile material would be routinely available in substantial amounts in states using such technologies, with the likely time between a decision to build a bomb and successful weaponization measured in weeks. To extend the delay to months, such reprocessing would need to be ended globally, and nuclear reactors of all types would have to eschew the use of fuel that is weapons grade in nature.

Experiments to improve verification of warhead and fissile stockpile inventories should be intensified as well, whether or not they are required for U.S. and Russian arms control per se. These experiments would be done partly to improve practices that will become even more important as stockpiles diminish further in subsequent arms accords.[58]

Taken together, a fissile cutoff treaty, HEU blend-down accords, and warhead dismantlement experiments will improve safety in the short term. Over the longer term, they will establish a growing international body of knowledge about the capabilities for verifying the close control of nuclear materials that will ultimately be needed to gauge the degree to which a nuclear disarmament accord can be monitored reasonably well.

Missile Defense

Missile defense has been among the most polarizing and contentious issues in U.S. defense policy for a quarter century. It remains so today. It will remain so as the United States pursues future arms control—not only the possibility of nuclear disarmament but the more immediate issue of a deep-cut regime that goes beyond the New START accord. Because of the proliferation of conventionally armed missiles, missile defense will remain a necessary priority for the United States with or without pursuit of nuclear disarmament, so the issue is very important and enduring.

The United States is fairly firmly set against limits on missile defenses. The Bush administration withdrew from the Anti-Ballistic Missile (ABM) Treaty in 2002 and proceeded to deploy ballistic missile defense systems—most notably one for intercepting long-range warheads in the midcourse of their flight. That system had originally been developed largely by the Clinton administration, which had an explicit option for deploying it even if negotiations with Russia to allow deployment under a possibly revised ABM Treaty failed. Thus, although the Bush administration was eager to withdraw from a treaty that the Clinton administration had very mixed views about, at some level the decision to deploy these missile defense systems had a certain bipartisan quality. To be sure, most Democrats objected to the way in which the Bush administration withdrew unilaterally and rather abruptly from the treaty. But few Democrats are proposing that the United States rejoin, and the Obama administration does not appear to support formal missile defense limits either. Too many missile threats, with nuclear and conventional warheads, of ballistic and cruise varieties, threaten American interests around the world to make any such treaty simple to negotiate or even to spell out.

Missile defense is controversial in part because of its great expense. During the Bush presidency, the cost of the overall program averaged about $12 billion a year (including defenses against shorter-range missiles). That administration's outgoing request for fiscal year 2009 was for $13 billion, and the longer-term plan projected spending of $62.5 billion over the following five years.[59] President Obama scaled these plans back, but annual expenses are still about $10 billion, and projected five-year costs remain more than $50 billion, well above the levels spent by the Reagan, George H. W. Bush, or Clinton administrations in real dollar terms.

Missile defense has been a sore point in the U.S.-Russian relationship, most specifically in recent years over the U.S. proposal to place missile defenses at sites in Poland and the Czech Republic (discussed in more detail below). President Obama made a good decision when he canceled those plans. But he may still deploy missile defenses in those countries later, and Russia may or may not cooperate in the effort, so we may now be enjoying at most a temporary and partial reprieve from the previous disputes caused by this matter rather than a permanent end to the problem.[60]

The missile defense issue also causes concerns in Beijing. Its nuclear arsenal is much smaller than Russia's and, in theory, could be countered to some extent by U.S. missile defenses. And China could conceivably wind up in a serious crisis with the United States over the matter of Taiwan (even if that seems less likely at the moment). One need not oppose missile defense categorically, wish for a restoration of the ABM Treaty, or sympathize with any and all criticisms of missile defense by foreign governments to recognize the sensitivities of the issue.

Several programs are at the core of the current U.S. missile defense effort. They include the Patriot missile (for a ground-based defense against missiles in the final or "terminal" stage of flight); THAAD (Theater High Altitude Area Defense, a ground-based defense against midcourse threats of modest range); the Alaska-California system (a ground-based defense, with help from sea-based radar, against long-range missile threats); and the Aegis Navy system (against missile threats over or near the sea, as well as a ground-based version to be developed). In addition, many of these specific systems are being linked together and fed information by various command and control systems, radar programs (upgrades to existing radars and deployment of new ones), and the planned launch of a major satellite constellation to track warheads (and try to identify them if disguised within clouds of decoys or other countermeasures). These various types of capabilities also are being upgraded more or less continuously.

At this point in mid-2010, the Missile Defense Agency has now upgraded land radars in Japan, the United Kingdom, Alaska, and California and built a sea-based mobile radar homeported in Alaska. Naval interceptors are fast improving too. Notably, several hundred launch tubes are in place on modern American Aegis destroyers and cruisers that could in theory house the Standard Missile-3 (SM-3) interceptor. That interceptor is one of a number of "hit to kill" interceptors that have been performing much better of late on test ranges.[61] Admittedly, not all tests have been realistic, and none has yet involved sophisticated decoys of the type an advanced power might be able to field. But further improvements are expected—for example, new missiles (one being developed with Japan) within the Navy SM-3 program that have a greater range and speed as well as more capable two-color, infrared sensors for tracking.[62]

Proponents of missile defense systems were often pilloried in the past for pursuing unrealistic technology and "rushing to failure." Technologies were too grandiose, such as proposals for giant lasers in space with their beams steered to targets by telescope-like mirrors, and too hurried, with programs structured on a crash basis. In recent years programs have been somewhat more realistic and also more successful, at least against simple threats.

Yet important questions remain about whether any missile defense system can really work against a sophisticated enemy. It would face two huge, inherent challenges under such circumstances: first, an attacker would not need to get all or even most nuclear-tipped missiles through a defense to be successful; and second, relatively simple countermeasures can mimic actual warheads or otherwise spoof sensors, making it very hard for a defense to know which incoming objects are true threats and which are not. While a defender can always develop methods of discrimination, attackers can always further improve the quality of their decoys, and on balance the interactions would seem to favor the attacker, especially in the vacuum of space where the weight of any warhead could not be easily used to distinguish it from a decoy. Beyond the issue of sophisticated decoys, missile defense systems to date have not been reliably proved to work at night or against a reentry vehicle that tumbles rather than falling straight (tumbling makes the flight less predictable) or against decoys even generally resembling real warheads.[63]

Still, it is not obvious that a less sophisticated and less wealthy country like North Korea could afford enough missile flight tests to perfect decoys. (In fact, in an otherwise successful test in 2008, the United States itself attempted to use countermeasures on a ballistic missile used as a target in a missile defense test, but the countermeasures failed to function properly.[64]) Nor, given the likely international political reaction, is it clear that rogue states could easily conduct such tests. Perhaps it will be possible to create an arms control regime in which, en route to zero, great powers do not feel threatened by each other's missile defenses, but the defenses create a growing capability that could represent a form of insurance against cheating by a smaller, rogue state under a nuclear disarmament accord. That is an optimistic vision of where technology might lead, but one worth pursuing.

In light of a missile defense's uncertain technical attributes, and the huge expense involved in purchasing multiple and redundant systems, the Obama administration was on reasonable footing in scaling back overall missile defense efforts. Its list of cutbacks included the airborne laser, which has demonstrated recent progress in several ground tests but is of uncertain near-term technological ripeness; the next round of planned expansions of the midcourse missile defense; and any advanced development of the kinetic energy interceptor missile.[65] Postponements should not necessarily be construed as "punishment" for poor performance; the airborne laser program, for example, appears to have progressed reasonably well before being effectively stopped by Secretary Gates.[66] Rather, at some point, the question becomes one of affordability and efficiency. A certain amount of redundancy is appropriate in missile defense, given the high stakes. In addition, the boost-phase kinetic energy interceptors were also accompanied by a strong program for improving command and control that would have benefits for other types of missile defense too, and those elements are worth continuing to research. But building THAAD and Navy Aegis and airborne laser systems all at once may verge on the excessive, solely on the grounds of budgetary and opportunity costs.

Even with such decisions, missile defense efforts will remain expensive, in the range of $10 billion a year instead of $12 billion to $13 billion. That is still well above the inflation-adjusted levels of the Reagan years, when the costs were in the range of $6 billion to $7 billion (in 2011 dollars).[67] So today's overall effort is still expensive, but some degree of fiscal discipline is being observed.

Consider the missile defense system proposed for Poland and the Czech Republic in more detail. The Bush administration during its last years in office promoted a new ballistic missile defense capability, complementing the one established in recent years in California and Alaska and working with somewhat similar technologies. It was intended primarily to protect Europe and the United States from missiles launched from the Middle East. It was, in principle, a worthy idea, but the military benefits in the short term were not worth the worsening of relations with Russia that it engendered. President Obama has been right to develop an alternative plan for deployment rather than rush to follow through on the previous schedule.

The proposed system would have consisted of a single radar on Czech soil and ten interceptor missiles in Poland. Many NATO states support the general idea of a missile defense system. Yet they wondered why Washington originally decided to pursue this plan primarily as a two-track process with only Poland and the Czech Republic—two new, modest-size members of the alliance— given the broader significance of a missile defense for NATO as a whole. A bigger question may be why the United States was in such a hurry to get this system going, especially given its inherent limitations. The ten interceptor missiles could in theory intercept only ten warheads and in all probability would do well to destroy a couple. Given the short amount of time available to destroy a missile launched from the Middle East—likely no more than twenty minutes—several of the defensive missiles would likely have to be fired at once to destroy a single warhead, because there would have been no time to wait and see if an initial interceptor hit its mark. In addition, the interceptors were based on technology that had not yet been proved fully reliable.

The flip side of the controversy over this proposed missile defense is that Russia's objections to it were without serious strategic merit.[68] Hypothetical arguments were made about these ten interceptors being able to knock down a couple of Russian warheads.[69] But these were badly exaggerated in Moscow in light of the small size of the intended deployment, the transparency that would accompany it (or any subsequent hypothetical addition to it), the vulnerability of such a system to the kinds of countermeasures that Russia could surely develop, and in a broader sense the obsolescence and essential irrelevance of the U.S.-Russian strategic competition. Russia will continue to have many hundreds of ballistic missile warheads if not more. Not to mention that Russia could do what a rogue regime might not have the technology to accomplish: deploy countermeasures that could make the small system entirely useless. For example, the antimissile program might well be fooled by missiles that release several decoys after they leave the atmosphere. The fact that Russia objected so strongly suggests that Moscow is a long way from being willing to stop using nuclear weapons issues as pawns in global power relations. That may bode badly for the future of the nuclear disarmament vision—at least under current Russian leaders.

But the fact of the matter is that Russia did object to the plan, many European allies were nervous, and the whole idea was associated with Bush administration unilateralism. Any major decision to build a new defense system needs to recognize these realities and factor them into the strategic and diplomatic calculus. President Obama was wise to authorize a more dispersed system using a range of technologies, many sea-based and not all to be based in former Warsaw Pact countries. The new plan will initially place interceptors on ships in the Mediterranean and later put adapted versions on land in places possibly ranging from Turkey and the Balkans to central Europe. The administration reserves the right to change its mind, as it should given the potential for changing technologies and changing threats.

Should the United States again attempt to address missile defense issues by treaty? The spat over a European-based defense may have been at least temporarily resolved, but, as noted, no agreement on a long-term approach has been reached, and the broader issue could easily interfere with future progress toward further arms control including nuclear disarmament. However, any treaty on defenses would be extremely hard to fashion given the technical reality that there are now many types of missile defense systems and that the lines between what were once called short-range and theater missile defenses, on the one hand, and national missile defenses, on the other, have been blurred. This is increasingly true not only for American systems but for those of Russia and some U.S. allies as well.[70]

The best approach would involve the sharing of information on planned systems, together with efforts to collaborate so that defenses would protect Russian as well as U.S.-NATO interests and involve the technologies and assets of both sides.[71] Whether or not he was fully sincere, Putin did show some flexibility in regard to the Europe-based missile defense issue, proposing joint development of a defense system that could make use of a Soviet-built radar in Azerbaijan and another on Russian territory. These ideas may be clever means of appearing reasonable without any real commitment to the notion of joint missile defense—but they are not unserious technically and are worth pursuing, at least as an element of a European defense system.[72] This kind of cooperation will clearly be needed before nuclear disarmament can ever be a serious prospect.

6 CONCLUSION

A GLOBAL ZERO ACCORD that would eliminate all nuclear weapons from the face of the Earth is one of the most challenging propositions ever conceived in international politics. It is far ahead of its time. Even to pursue it seriously would be counterproductive, perhaps fostering the very nuclear proliferation dynamics that it would be designed in large part to counter. It would almost certainly never be truly verifiable, given the rigor required for such an absolutist accord. It would not necessarily be permanent, despite the hopes and expectations of its most fervent advocates. It would not necessarily limit the possible future use of a country's nuclear arsenal to the sole purpose of deterring nuclear attacks by others, particularly given the potential for a future aggressor state to develop advanced biological pathogens. In other words, a nuclear disarmament treaty would be saddled with limitations, caveats, and uncertainties.

And yet, such an accord is a very good idea. That is, nuclear disarmament is a worthwhile goal for the international community to adopt seriously. President Obama was right to give a major speech on the subject early in his presidency; other world leaders have been right to promote the idea as well. Obama and others should continue to look for meaningful and pragmatic, measured ways to advance the idea of eliminating nuclear weapons even now that many of the initial, lofty speeches have been delivered and the grandiose goals articulated.

The objective of eliminating nuclear weapons has been stated American policy since the Johnson administration. It is a core element of the Nuclear Non-Proliferation Treaty and the basic bargain in that 1968 accord between nuclear and nonnuclear states. In that regard, recent attention to the subject merely reiterates what has been U.S. policy for every U.S. president between Johnson and Obama—Nixon, Ford, Carter, Reagan, the first Bush, Clinton, and the second Bush.

Critics and skeptics are generally correct in their doubts about a nuclear abolition treaty. They are egged on by treaty advocates who often make challenges to aspects of such a regime seem straightforward to surmount when in fact they are not. For example, the notion that the United States has such overwhelming conventional military dominance as to make threats such as those posed by weapons of mass destruction superfluous is belied by the experiences in Iraq and Afghanistan this decade, not to mention centuries of military history (and common sense).

The challenges to achieving a nuclear disarmament treaty are enormous. The world is nowhere near ready for such an accord to be negotiated. Great-power relations need to be stabilized, major irredentist issues from Taiwan to Kashmir to the Middle East and the Caucasus resolved, and further measures to monitor arms control accords honed before any treaty-writing process should begin. And, of course, we are probably decades away from a world in which *all* known and suspected nuclear powers would actually sign up to such a treaty—a necessary precondition for *any* of them to implement it.

But despite all the impediments, a way ahead can be seen. The effort to eliminate nuclear weapons can never move too far ahead of the state of world politics more generally, but it can be a useful complement to other measures that include old-fashioned military deterrence and at times the actual use of military force to create a more stable and just international order. And real things can be done, in terms of arms control, military doctrine, and approaches to offensive nuclear arms control as well as deployment of future missile defenses, that not only would be influenced by the nuclear disarmament agenda but would also perhaps serve to advance that agenda.

It is too soon to know if nuclear disarmament will be possible; even if a disarmament is achieved, it may not endure forever, and a great deal of attention must be devoted to the reconstitution issue, as this book has attempted to do. But the destructiveness of these weapons, and the likelihood that they cannot forever be safely maintained, deployed, and otherwise utilized as normal currency in international politics, makes it unwise to get too used to them. They are horrible instruments of death, not respectable and usable weapons, and we need to seek a world that puts them in their proper place.

NOTES

Chapter One

1. See for example, Ivo Daalder and Jan Lodal, "The Logic of Zero," *Foreign Affairs* 87 (November-December 2008).

2. "Global Zero" (www.globalzero.org/en/getting-zero [April 5, 2010]).

3. Richard Butler, *The Greatest Threat: Iraq, Weapons of Mass Destruction, and the Growing Crisis of Global Security* (New York: Public Affairs, 2000), pp. 32–33.

4. See, for example, Jonathan Schell, *The Fate of the Earth* (New York: Alfred A. Knopf, 1982), pp. 181–84.

5. Robert M. Gates, *Nuclear Posture Review Report* (Department of Defense, April 2010). In actual terms, the reductions in deployed long-range warhead counts will apparently be about 10 percent or perhaps slightly more. See Union of Concerned Scientists, "Fact Sheet: New START Treaty" (Cambridge, Mass.: April 2, 2010) (www.ucsusa.org/assets/documents/nwgs/start-follow-on-fact-sheet.pdf [April 16, 2010]).

6. For a good argument along these lines, see Peter D. Feaver, "Obama's Nuclear Modesty," *New York Times,* April 9, 2010.

7. White House, "Highlights of the National Commitments Made at the Nuclear Security Summit," April 12–13, 2010 (www.whitehouse.gov/the-press-office/highlights-national-commitments-made-nss [April 15, 2010]).

8. Gates, *Nuclear Posture Review Report,* p. 11.

9. Some critics of nuclear zero contest the notion that taking away such an excuse could be reason enough to pursue nuclear disarmament—and they are right to do so. See for example Douglas J. Feith and Abram N. Shulsky, "The Dangerous Illusion of 'Nuclear Zero,'" *Wall Street Journal*, May 21, 2010, p. A15; and Bruno Tertrais, "The Illogic of Zero," *Washington Quarterly*, vol. 33 (April 2010), pp. 129–30.

10. Sam Nunn, "Taking Steps toward a World Free of Nuclear Weapons," *Daedalus* (Fall 2009), p. 155.

11. Gates, *Nuclear Posture Review Report*, p. 16.

12. See, for example, Fred C. Ikle, "Nuclear Abolition, A Reverie," *National Interest*, no. 103 (September-October 2009), p. 6.

13. United Nations, "2010 Review Conference of the Parties to the Treaty on the Non-Proliferation of Nuclear Weapons (NPT)" (New York: 2010) (www.un.org/en/conf/npt/2010/background.shtml [April 5, 2010]).

14. John Mueller, *Atomic Obsession: Nuclear Alarmism from Hiroshima to al-Qaeda* (Oxford University Press, 2010), pp. 129–58.

15. Alexei G. Arbatov, "Russian Nuclear Posture: Capabilities, Missions, and Mysteries inside Enigmas," paper presented at Stanford University conference "P-5 Nuclear Doctrines and Article VI," October 16–17, 2007, p. 120.

16. For a discussion of the second nuclear age, see Robert P. Haffa Jr., Ravi R. Hichkad, Dana J. Johnson, and Philip W. Pratt, "Deterrence and Defense in 'The Second Nuclear Age'" (Arlington, Va.: Northrop Grumman Analysis Center, 2007), pp. 5–11 (www.analysiscenter.northrop grumman.com [September 1, 2009]). For another discussion of extended deterrence, see Andrew F. Krepinevich, *U.S. Nuclear Forces: Meeting the Challenge of a Proliferated World* (Washington: Center for Strategic and Budgetary Assessments, 2009).

17. Bruce Riedel, "Pakistan and the Bomb," *Wall Street Journal*, May 30, 2009 (online.wsj.com/article/SB100014240529702036585045741918 42820382548.html [July 2, 2009]).

18. Michael O'Hanlon, *Technological Change and the Future of Warfare* (Brookings, 2000), pp. 144–53.

19. For a concurring view on this point, see Sverre Lodgaard, "Toward a Nuclear-Weapons-Free World," *Daedalus* (Fall 2009), p. 142.

20. Defense against asteroids that threaten to crash into Earth is a very remote, but not totally absurd, additional possibility that could lead to a need for a short-term reconstitution of a nuclear capability—if not by a single country, then by the international community writ large.

However, it is not at the center of any argument I make in this book. For a credible and readable account, see Caryn Meissner, "Too Close for Comfort," *Science and Technology Review* (December 2009), pp. 12–14.

Chapter Two

1. Ronald E. Powaski, *March to Armageddon* (Oxford University Press, 1987), pp. 3–28.

2. Richard Falk, "Non-Proliferation Treaty Illusions and International Lawlessness," in *At the Nuclear Precipice: Catastrophe or Transformation?* edited by Richard Falk and David Krieger (New York: Palgrave Macmillan, 2008), pp. 39–47.

3. Kenneth N. Waltz, "Nuclear Myths and Political Realities," in *The Use of Force: Military Power and International Politics*, 6th ed., edited by Robert J. Art and Kenneth N. Waltz (New York: Rowman and Littlefield Publishers, 2004), pp. 102–17.

4. T. V. Paul, *The Tradition of Non-Use of Nuclear Weapons* (Stanford University Press, 2009), pp. 199–208.

5. McGeorge Bundy, *Danger and Survival: Choices about the Bomb in the First Fifty Years* (New York: Vintage Books, 1988), pp. 461–62; Michael Dobbs, *One Minute to Midnight* (New York: Alfred A. Knopf, 2008), p. xiv.

6. Bundy, *Danger and Survival*, p. 462.

7. Dobbs, *One Minute to Midnight*, p. 351.

8. See also Neil Sheehan, *A Fiery Peace in a Cold War: Bernard Schriever and the Ultimate Weapon* (New York: Random House, 2009), pp. 442–46.

9. Richard K. Betts, *Nuclear Blackmail and Nuclear Balance* (Brookings, 1987), p. xi.

10. Lawrence Freedman, *The Evolution of Nuclear Strategy* (New York: St. Martin's Press, 1981), pp. 76–90.

11. Betts, *Nuclear Blackmail and Nuclear Balance*, pp. 92–109.

12. Fred Kaplan, "JFK's First-Strike Plan," *Atlantic Monthly*, October 2001 (www.theatlantic.com/past/issues/2001/10/kaplan.htm [April 5, 2010]).

13. McNamara quoted in John Newhouse, *The Nuclear Age: From Hiroshima to Star Wars* (London: Michael Joseph, 1989), p. 157.

14. Victor D. Cha, "Hawk Engagement and Preventive Defense on the Korean Peninsula," *International Security* 27 (Summer 2002), pp. 40–48.

15. Robert Jervis, "The Utility of Nuclear Deterrence," in *The Use of Force: Military Power and International Politics*, edited by Art and Waltz, p. 100.

16. For perspective on Kahn's escalation ladder, including discussion of Kahn's book *On Escalation*, see Lawrence Freedman, *The Evolution of Nuclear Strategy* (New York: St. Martin's Press, 1983), pp. 215–19; for other aspects of Kahn's thinking, see Herman Kahn, *On Thermonuclear War* (New Brunswick, N.J.: Transaction Publishers, 2007), esp. pp. 3–39.

17. Thomas C. Schelling, *The Strategy of Conflict*, 1980 ed. (Harvard University Press, 2002), pp. 187–203.

18. Bernard Brodie, *Strategy in the Missile Age* (Princeton University Press, 1971), p. 391.

19. Paul, *The Tradition of Non-Use of Nuclear Weapons*, pp. 127–29.

20. Strobe Talbott, *Engaging India: Diplomacy, Democracy, and the Bomb*, rev. ed. (Brookings, 2006), pp. 154–69; and Stephen Philip Cohen, *India: Emerging Power* (Brookings, 2001), pp. 185–86.

21. Michael Quinlan, *Thinking about Nuclear Weapons: Principles, Problems, Prospects* (Oxford University Press, 2009), p. 135.

22. Kurt M. Campbell, Robert J. Einhorn, and Mitchell B. Reiss, eds., *The Nuclear Tipping Point* (Brookings, 2004).

23. Richard K. Betts, "Universal Deterrence or Conceptual Collapse? Liberal Pessimism and Utopian Realism," in *The Coming Crisis: Nuclear Proliferation, U.S. Interests, and World Order*, edited by Victor A. Utgoff (MIT Press, 2000), p. 72.

24. Freeman Dyson, *Weapons and Hope* (New York: Harpercollins, 1984), p. 461.

25. Scott D. Sagan, *The Limits of Safety: Organizations, Accidents, and Nuclear Weapons* (Princeton University Press, 1993), p. 3.

26. Ibid., pp. 78–80, 135–38.

27. Ibid., pp. 156–57, 178, 188, 202.

28. Ibid., pp. 225–33.

29. Secretary of Defense Task Force, *Report of the Secretary of Defense Task Force on DoD Nuclear Weapons Management, Phase I: The Air Force's Nuclear Mission* (Washington: September 2008), p. 13 (www.defense.gov/pubs/Phase_I_Report_Sept_10.pdf [December 7, 2009]).

30. Bruce G. Blair, *Strategic Command and Control: Redefining the Nuclear Threat* (Brookings, 1985), pp. 5, 285.

31. David E. Hoffman, *The Dead Hand: The Untold Story of the Cold War Arms Race and Its Dangerous Legacy* (New York: Doubleday, 2009).

32. Barry R. Posen, *Inadvertent Escalation: Conventional War and Nuclear Risks* (Cornell University Press, 1991), pp. 15–16.

33. On surprise attack, see Richard K. Betts, *Surprise Attack* (Brookings, 1982), pp. 3–10.

34. See Janne E. Nolan, *Guardians of the Arsenal: The Politics of Nuclear Strategy* (New York: Basic Books, 1989).

35. Bruce G. Blair, *Global Zero Alert for Nuclear Forces* (Brookings, 1995), pp. 20, 46–48.

36. Brian Michael Jenkins, *Will Terrorists Go Nuclear?* (New York: Prometheus Books, 2008), p. 368.

37. John McPhee, *The Curve of Binding Energy* (New York: Farrar, Straus, and Giroux, 1973), p. 124.

38. George Tenet, *At the Center of the Storm: My Years at the CIA* (New York: HarperCollins, 2007), pp. 102, 260–62; Bruce Riedel, *The Search for al Qaeda: Its Leadership, Ideology, and Future* (Brookings, 2008), p. 133.

39. Michael Levi, *On Nuclear Terrorism* (Harvard University Press, 2007), pp. 49–61.

40. Peter Crail, "Pakistani Nuclear Stocks Safe, Officials Say," *Arms Control Today* 39 (June 2009), p. 29.

41. Feroz Hassan Khan, "Nuclear Security in Pakistan: Separating Myth from Reality," *Arms Control Today* 39 (July/August 2009), p. 19; Rolf Mowatt-Larssen, "Nuclear Security in Pakistan: Reducing the Risks of Nuclear Terrorism," *Arms Control Today* 39 (July/August 2009), pp. 9–11.

42. Graham Allison, *Nuclear Terrorism: The Ultimate Preventable Catastrophe* (New York: Times Books, 2004), pp. 64–67, 82–85.

43. Jenkins, *Will Terrorists Go Nuclear?* pp. 171–79.

44. Allison, *Nuclear Terrorism: The Ultimate Preventable Catastrophe*, p. 15.

45. Andrew Newman and Matthew Bunn, "Funding for U.S. Efforts to Improve Controls over Nuclear Weapons, Materials, and Expertise Overseas: A 2009 Update," Project on Managing the Atom (Harvard University, Belfer Center for Science and International Affairs, June 2009), pp. 1-4; and Matthew Bunn, *Securing the Bomb 2008* (Harvard University, Belfer Center for Science and International Affairs, and

Washington: Nuclear Threat Initiative, November 2008), pp. 8–9, 51, 96–104 (www.nti.org/securingthebomb [December 3, 2009]).

46. See, for example, Gordon Corera, *Shopping for Bombs: Nuclear Proliferation, Global Insecurity, and the Rise and Fall of the A. Q. Khan Network* (Oxford University Press, 2006), pp. 219–39.

47. Anna Wetter, *Enforcing European Union Law on Exports of Dual-Use Goods* (Oxford University Press, 2009), pp. 1–9, 89–136.

48. See, for example, Harold Feiveson, "A Skeptic's View of Nuclear Energy," *Daedalus* (Fall 2009), pp. 60–70.

49. Sharon Squassoni, *Nuclear Energy: Rebirth or Resuscitation?* (Washington: Carnegie Endowment, 2009), pp. 55–57.

50. Sharon Squassoni, "Nuclear Renaissance: Is It Coming? Should It?" (Washington: Carnegie Endowment, October 2008), p. 4; Ux Consulting, "Uranium Market Outlook: A Market in Transition" (Roswell, Ga.: 2009) (www.uxc.com [December 3, 2009].

51. On Poland, see Barry M. Blechman, "Why We Need to Eliminate Nuclear Weapons—And How to Do It," in *Elements of a Nuclear Disarmament Treaty*, edited by Barry M. Blechman and Alexander K. Bollfrass (Washington: Henry L. Stimson Center, 2010), p. 4.

52. Jonathan Schell, "The Power of Abolition," in *Abolishing Nuclear Weapons: A Debate*, edited by George Perkovich and James M. Acton (Washington: Carnegie Endowment, 2009), p. 161.

Chapter Three

1. Charles L. Glaser, "The Flawed Case for Nuclear Disarmament," *Survival* 40 (Spring 1998), pp. 112–28.

2. John Mueller, "The Essential Irrelevance of Nuclear Weapons: Stability in the Postwar World," *International Security* 13 (Fall 1988), pp. 55–79.

3. For a somewhat different view, see Frank Miller, "Disarmament and Deterrence: A Practitioner's View," in *Abolishing Nuclear Weapons: A Debate*, edited by George Perkovich and James M. Acton (Washington: Carnegie Endowment, 2009), p. 151.

4. Ward Wilson, "The Winning Weapon? Rethinking Nuclear Weapons In Light of Hiroshima," *International Security* 31 (Spring 2007), pp. 162–79.

5. Steve Fetter and Ivan Oelrich, "Verifying a Prohibition on Nuclear Weapons," in *Elements of a Nuclear Disarmament Treaty*, edited by

Barry M. Blechman and Alexander K. Bollfrass (Washington: Henry L. Stimson Center, 2010), p. 30.

6. Ivo H. Daalder and Michael E. O'Hanlon, *Winning Ugly: NATO's War to Save Kosovo* (Brookings, 2000); Benjamin S. Lambeth, *NATO's Air War for Kosovo: A Strategic and Operational Assessment* (Santa Monica, Calif.: RAND, 2001), pp. 67–86.

7. Katie Walter, "The Hunt for Better Radiation Detection," *Science and Technology Review* (January-February 2010), pp. 4–10.

8. Michael Levi, *On Nuclear Terrorism* (Harvard University Press, 2007), pp. 52–61.

9. David E. Sanger and William J. Broad, "U.S. and Allies Warn Iran over 'Nuclear Deception,'" *New York Times,* September 26, 2009, p. 1.

10. See, for example, Hans Blix, *Disarming Iraq* (New York: Pantheon Books, 2004), pp. 23–24.

11. Sharon Squassoni, *Nuclear Energy: Rebirth or Resuscitation?* (Washington: Carnegie Endowment, 2009), pp. 9, 50–59.

12. Mohamed El Baradei, "Saving Ourselves from Self-Destruction," *New York Times,* February 12, 2004.

13. Harold A. Feiveson, "Civilian Nuclear Power in a Nuclear-Weapon-Free World," in *Elements of a Nuclear Disarmament Treaty,* edited by Blechman and Bollfrass, p. 73.

14. Michael Levi and Michael E. O'Hanlon, *The Future of Arms Control* (Brookings, 2005), pp. 58–63.

15. International Panel on Fissile Materials, "Global Fissile Material Report 2009: A Path to Nuclear Disarmament" (New York: 2009), p. 7 (www.fissilematerials.org [April 5, 2010]).

16. George Perkovich and James M. Acton, *Abolishing Nuclear Weapons,* Adelphi Paper 396 (London: International Institute for Strategic Studies, 2008), p. 56.

17. International Panel on Fissile Materials, "Global Fissile Material Report 2009," pp. 21–22.

18. George Bunn and Christopher F. Chyba, "U.S. Nuclear Weapons Policies for a New Era," in *U.S. Nuclear Weapons Policy: Confronting Today's Threats,* edited by George Bunn and Christopher F. Chyba (Brookings, 2006), p. 314.

19. Jean du Preez, "A South African Perspective on the Nuclear Postures of the Five NPT Nuclear Weapons States," paper presented at Stanford University conference "P-5 Nuclear Doctrines and Article VI" (October 16–17, 2007), p. 160.

20. Patrick M. Cronin, ed., *Global Strategic Assessment 2009: America's Security Role in a Changing World* (Washington: Institute for National Strategic Studies, National Defense University, 2009), p. 181.

21. Harold A. Feiveson, Bruce G. Blair, Jonathan Dean, Steve Fetter, James Goodby, George N. Lewis, Janne E. Nolan, Theodore Postol, and Frank von Hippel, *The Nuclear Turning Point: A Blueprint for Deep Cuts and De-Alerting of Nuclear Weapons* (Brookings, 1999), p. 36.

22. John D. Steinbruner and Elisa D. Harris, "Controlling Dangerous Pathogens," *Issues in Science and Technology* (Spring 2003), p. 52.

23. Michael Moodie, Cheryl Loeb, Robert Armstrong, and Helen Purkitt, "Good Bugs, Bad Bugs: A Modern Approach for Detecting Offensive Biological Weapons Research," Defense and Technology Paper 54 (Washington: Center for Technology and National Security Policy, National Defense University, September 2008), p. v.

24. Newt Gingrich, George Mitchell, and the Independent Task Force on the United Nations, *American Interests and U.N. Reform* (Washington: U.S. Institute of Peace, 2005), p. 83.

25. Mark Wheelis, "Biotechnology and Biochemical Weapons," *Nonproliferation Review* (Spring 2002), pp. 48–53; Levi and O'Hanlon, *The Future of Arms Control*, pp. 76–77.

26. Levi and O'Hanlon, *The Future of Arms Control*, pp. 75–86.

27. See, for example, Carina Dennis, "The Bugs of War," *Nature*, no. 411 (May 17, 2001), pp. 232–35 (www.nature.com [January 1, 2007]).

28. John D. Steinbruner, *Principles of Global Security* (Brookings, 2000), p. 178.

29. Gail H. Cassell, "Countermeasures to Biological Threats: The Challenges of Drug Development," in *Biological Threats and Terrorism: Assessing the Science and Response Capabilities*, edited by Stacey L. Knobler, Adel A. F. Mahmoud, and Leslie A. Pray (Washington: National Academies Press, 2002), pp. 115–16.

30. Gregory D. Koblentz and Jonathan B. Tucker, "Tracing an Attack: The Promise and Pitfalls of Microbial Forensics," *Survival* 52 (February–March 2010), pp. 159–85.

31. Keith B. Payne, "On Nuclear Deterrence and Assurance," *Strategic Studies Quarterly* 3 (Spring 2009), p. 45.

32. Michael Walzer, *Just and Unjust Wars: A Moral Argument with Historical Illustrations* (New York: Basic Books, 1977), pp. 269–83.

33. See Payne, "On Nuclear Deterrence and Assurance," p. 59, for a discussion of the potential utility of smaller and possibly more accurate

nuclear weapons. Today's weapons might be used not only in more remote locations but in other locations if other steps were also taken, such as giving populations warning of imminent attacks near cities, or detonating warheads higher in the atmosphere than would normally be considered "optimal" depending on the specifics of the situation.

34. Steinbruner, *Principles of Global Security*, p. 180.

35. See, for example, "Getting to Zero: An Interview with International Nuclear Non-Proliferation and Disarmament Commission Co-Chair Gareth Evans," *Arms Control Today* 39 (April 2009), p. 8.

36. Payne, "On Nuclear Deterrence and Assurance," p. 49.

37. Scott D. Sagan, "The Commitment Trap: Why the United States Should Not Use Nuclear Threats to Deter Biological and Chemical Weapons Attacks," *International Security* 24 (Spring 2000), pp. 85–115.

38. Stephen I. Schwartz, "Introduction," in *Atomic Audit: The Costs and Consequences of U.S. Nuclear Weapons Since 1940,* edited by Stephen I. Schwartz (Brookings, 1998), pp. 1–3.

39. Stephen I. Schwartz with Deepti Choubey, *Nuclear Security Spending: Assessing Costs, Examining Priorities* (Washington: Carnegie Endowment, 2009), pp. 18–33.

40. Congressional Budget Office, *The START Treaty and Beyond* (Washington: 1992), p. 62.

41. Gu Guoliang, "China's Nuclear Posture and Article VI," paper presented at Stanford University conference "P-5 Nuclear Doctrines and Article VI" (October 16–17, 2007), p. 185; Bates Gill, *Rising Star: China's New Security Diplomacy* (Brookings, 2007), pp. 98–103.

42. Geoffrey Blainey, *The Causes of War* (New York: Free Press, 1973), pp. 246–49.

43. By "roughly comparable military capabilities," I mean a situation in which neither side is estimated to exceed the other's capabilities by more than 50 percent. See Requirements and Resources Directorate, U.S. Army Concepts Analysis Agency, *Combat History Analysis Study Effort (CHASE): Progress Report* (Washington: Army Concepts Analysis Agency, 1986), pp. 3–20, cited in Joshua M. Epstein, "Dynamic Analysis and the Conventional Balance in Europe," *International Security* 12 (Spring 1988), p. 156.

44. Richard K. Betts, *Surprise Attack* (Brookings, 1982), pp. 5–16.

45. Epstein, "Dynamic Analysis and the Conventional Balance in Europe," p. 156.

46. See also Stephen Biddle, *Military Power* (Princeton University Press, 1984).

47. Rachel Schmidt, *Moving U.S. Forces: Options for Strategic Mobility* (Congressional Budget Office, 1997), pp. 48, 54, 80–81; Department of Defense, *Conduct of the Persian Gulf War: Final Report to Congress* (April 1992), p. F-26.

48. David Arthur, *Options for Strategic Military Transportation Systems* (Congressional Budget Office, September 2005), pp. x, xii, 3, 5.

49. National Defense Panel, *Transforming Defense: National Security in the 21st Century* (Washington: 1997), pp. 7–8.

50. Ronald O'Rourke, *Navy Ship Propulsion Technologies: Options for Reducing Oil Use* (Congressional Research Service, 2006), pp. 1–10 (fas.org/sgp/crs/weapons/RL33360.pdf [April 11, 2008]).

51. For a concurring view, see John Lyons, Richard Chait, and Jordan Willcox, *An Assessment of the Science and Technology Predictions in the Army's STAR21 Report* (Washington: Center for Technology and National Security Policy, National Defense University, July 2008), p. 23.

52. Robert H. Scales Jr., "Cycles of War: Speed of Maneuver Will Be the Essential Ingredient of an Information-Age Army," *Armed Forces Journal International* 134 (July 1997), p. 38.

53. Eric V. Larson, *Casualties and Consensus* (Santa Monica, Calif.: RAND, 1996).

54. Iida Masafumi, "New Developments in China's Policy on the South China Sea," *NIDS Security Reports*, no. 9 (December 2008), pp. 3–16.

55. Maria Rost Rublee, *Nonproliferation Norms: Why States Choose Nuclear Restraint* (University of Georgia Press, 2009), p. 222.

56. See, for example, David N. Schwartz, *NATO's Nuclear Dilemmas* (Brookings, 1983), p. 12.

57. Christopher W. Hughes, *Japan's Remilitarisation* (London: International Institute for Strategic Studies, 2009), pp. 102–12; Michael J. Green and Katsuhisa Furukawa, "Japan: New Nuclear Realism," in *The Long Shadow: Nuclear Weapons and Security in 21st Century Asia*, edited by Muthiah Alagappa (Stanford University Press, 2008), pp. 347–71.

58. Morihiro Hosokawa, "Are U.S. Troops in Japan Needed? Reforming the Alliance," *Foreign Affairs* 77 (July-August 1998), p. 5.

59. Masa Takubo, "The Role of Nuclear Weapons: Japan, the U.S., and 'Sole Purpose,'" *Arms Control Today* 39 (November 2009), pp. 14–20.

60. Jonathan D. Pollack and Mitchell B. Reiss, "South Korea: The Tyranny of Geography and the Vexations of History," in *The Nuclear Tipping Point*, edited by Kurt M. Campbell, Robert J. Einhorn, and Mitchell B. Reiss (Brookings, 2004), pp. 261–65.

61. Payne, "On Nuclear Deterrence and Assurance," pp. 54–55.

62. Derek J. Mitchell, "Taiwan's Hsin Chu Program: Deterrence, Abandonment, and Honor," in *The Nuclear Tipping Point,* edited by Campbell, Einhorn, and Reiss, pp. 296–301.

63. Pollack and Reiss, "South Korea," in *The Nuclear Tipping Point,* edited by Campbell, Einhorn, and Reiss, p. 286.

64. Mitchell, "Taiwan's Hsin Chu Program," pp. 303, 309.

65. Catherine M. Kelleher and Scott L. Warren, "Getting to Zero Starts Here: Tactical Nuclear Weapons," *Arms Control Today* 39 (October 2009), p. 10; Robert J. Einhorn, "Egypt: Frustrated but Still on a Non-Nuclear Course," Thomas W. Lippman, "Saudi Arabia: The Calculations of Uncertainty," and Leon Fuerth, "Turkey: Nuclear Choices amongst Dangerous Neighbors," all in *The Nuclear Tipping Point,* edited by Campbell, Einhorn, and Reiss, pp. 45–51, 71, 134–138, and 145–174.

66. Martin Indyk and Tamara Cofman Wittes, "Back to Balancing in the Middle East: A New Strategy for Constructive Engagement," in *Opportunity 08: Independent Ideas for America's Next President,* edited by Michael E. O'Hanlon (Brookings, 2008), p. 123 ; and Steven Pifer, Richard C. Bush, Vanda Felbab-Brown, Martin S. Indyk, Michael O'Hanlon, and Kenneth M. Pollack, "U.S. Nuclear and Extended Deterrence: Considerations and Challenges," Arms Control Series Paper 3 (Brookings, 2010), pp. 39–45.

67. Rachel Bronson, *Thicker Than Oil: America's Uneasy Partnership with Saudi Arabia* (Oxford University Press, 2006), pp. 150–51, 252–54.

68. David Cortright and Raimo Vayrynen, *Towards Nuclear Zero* (London: International Institute for Strategic Studies, 2010), pp. 49–69.

69. Agence France-Presse, "Russia Plans Shift in Nuclear Doctrine: Reports," October 8, 2009 (www.afp.com).

70. Ariel E. Levite, "Global Zero: An Israeli Vision of Realistic Idealism," *Washington Quarterly* 33 (April 2010), pp. 157–68.

71. See, for example, Karim Sadjadpour, *Reading Khamenei: The World View of Iran's Most Powerful Leader* (Washington: Carnegie Endowment, 2008), pp. 19–21.

72. Vitaly Naumkin, Gennady Evstafiev, and Vladimir Novikov, "The Middle East," in *Nuclear Weapons after the Cold War,* edited by Alexei Arbatov and Vladimir Dvorkin (Washington: Carnegie Endowment, 2008), pp. 419–22.

73. Shlomo Brom, "Israeli Perspectives on the Global Elimination of Nuclear Weapons," in *Pakistan and Israel,* edited by Barry M. Blechman

(Washington: Henry L. Stimson Center, April 2009), pp. 37–59 (www.stimson.org/nuke/pdf/PAKISTAN_ISRAEL.pdf [July 31, 2009]).

74. Deepti Choubey, "Understanding the 2010 NPT Review Conference" (Washington: Carnegie Endowment, June 3, 2010) (www.carnegie endowment.org/publications/index.cfm?fa=view&id=40910 [June 4, 2010]).

75. Payne, "On Nuclear Deterrence and Assurance," pp. 61–62.

76. Bruno Tertrais, "French Perspectives on Nuclear Weapons and Nuclear Disarmament," and Lawrence Freedman, "British Perspectives on Nuclear Weapons and Nuclear Disarmament," in *Perspectives of Advanced Nuclear Nations,* edited by Barry M. Blechman, pp. 1–22, 23–61 (Washington: Henry L. Stimson Center, February 2009) (www.stimson.org/nuke/pdf/Nuclear_Security_FINAL_Complete_pdf.pdf [May 1, 2009]).

Chapter Four

1. Michael Krepon, *Better Safe than Sorry: The Ironies of Living with the Bomb* (Stanford University Press, 2009), p. 200.

2. For a similar argument, see Barry M. Blechman, "Why We Need to Eliminate Nuclear Weapons—And How to Do It," in *Elements of a Nuclear Disarmament Treaty,* edited by Barry M. Blechman and Alexander K. Bollfrass (Washington: Henry L. Stimson Center, 2010), pp. 11–13.

3. For more on North Korea, see Leon V. Sigal and Joel Wit, "North Korea's Perspectives on the Global Elimination of Nuclear Weapons," in *North Korea and Iran: Unblocking the Road to Zero,* edited by Barry M. Blechman (Washington: Henry L. Stimson Center, May 2009), p. 15 (www.stimson.org/nuke/pdf/NK_IRAN_FINAL.pdf [July 1, 2009]).

4. For a good discussion of this point, see Brad Roberts, "The Nuclear Dimension: How Likely? How Stable?" in *Assessing the Threat: The Chinese Military and Taiwan's Security,* edited by Michael D. Swaine, Andrew N. D. Yang, Evan S. Medeiros, and Oriana Skylar Mastro (Washington: Carnegie Endowment, 2007), pp. 213–31; Larry M. Wortzel, *China's Nuclear Forces: Operations, Training, Doctrine, Command, Control, and Campaign Planning* (Carlisle, Pa.: Strategic Studies Institute, Army War College, May 2007 (www.StrategicStudies Institute.army.mil [December 2, 2009]); Michael S. Chase, Andrew S. Erickson, and Christopher Yeaw, "Chinese Theater and Strategic Missile

Force Modernization and Its Implications for the United States," *Journal of Strategic Studies* 32 (February 2009), pp. 67–114; and Michael S. Chase and Evan Medeiros, "China's Evolving Nuclear Calculus: Modernization and Doctrinal Debate," in *China's Revolution in Doctrinal Affairs: Emerging Trends in the Operational Art of the Chinese People's Liberation Army,* edited by James Mulvenon and David Finkelstein (Alexandria, Va.: CNA Corporation, 2005), pp. 119–57.

5. Nikolai N. Sokov, "The Evolving Role of Nuclear Weapons in Russia's Security Policy," in *Engaging China and Russia on Nuclear Disarmament,* edited by Cristina Hansell and William C. Potter (Monterey, Calif.: Monterey Institute of International Studies, 2009), pp. 87–88.

6. For a similar argument, see Brad Roberts, "On Order, Stability, and Nuclear Abolition," in *Abolishing Nuclear Weapons: A Debate,* edited by George Perkovich and James M. Acton (Washington: Carnegie Endowment, 2009), pp. 163–64.

7. Thom Shanker, "Gates Gives Rationale for Expanded Deterrence," *New York Times,* October 29, 2008, p. A12.

8. Blechman, "Why We Need to Eliminate Nuclear Weapons—And How to Do It," pp. 11–20.

9. Richard L. Garwin and Georges Charpak, *Megawatts and Megatons: A Turning Point in the Nuclear Age?* (New York: Alfred A. Knopf, 2001), pp. 311–20, 361–75.

10. Steve Fetter and Ivan Oelrich, "Verifying a Prohibition on Nuclear Weapons," in *Elements of a Nuclear Disarmament Treaty,* edited by Blechman and Bollfrass, pp. 33–34.

11. International Atomic Energy Agency, "Fact Sheet: Program and Budget for 2010" (Vienna: 2009) (www.iaea.org/About/budget.html [December 6, 2009]).

12. Gregory L. Schulte, "Strengthening the IAEA: How the Nuclear Watchdog Can Regain Its Bark," *Strategic Forum* 253 (March 2010) (www.ndu.edu/inss [April 2, 2010]).

13. George Perkovich and James M. Acton, *Abolishing Nuclear Weapons,* Adelphi Paper 396 (London: International Institute for Strategic Studies, 2008), pp. 92–94.

14. Hans Blix, *Why Nuclear Disarmament Matters* (MIT Press, 2008), pp. 62–73.

15. Graham Allison, *Nuclear Terrorism: The Ultimate Preventable Catastrophe* (New York: Henry Holt and Company, 2004), pp. 187–92.

16. Harold A. Feiveson, Bruce G. Blair, Jonathan Dean, Steve Fetter, James Goodby, George N. Lewis, Janne E. Nolan, Theodore Postol, and Frank N. von Hippel, *The Nuclear Turning Point: A Blueprint for Deep Cuts and De-Alerting of Nuclear Weapons* (Brookings, 1999), p. 223.

17. For a related argument, see Perkovich and Acton, *Abolishing Nuclear Weapons*, pp. 100–01.

18. See, for example, Richard N. Haass, *War of Necessity, War of Choice* (New York: Simon and Schuster, 2010), pp. 230–31.

19. David Albright, Paul Brannan, and Andrea Scheel Stricker, "Detecting and Disrupting Illicit Nuclear Trade after A.Q. Khan," *Washington Quarterly* 33 (April 2010), pp. 101–04.

20. I am indebted to Jason Mehta for considerable help in understanding the legal aspects of treaty withdrawal clauses and options.

21. Perkovich and Acton, *Abolishing Nuclear Weapons,* pp. 92–95; for a related discussion on the Nuclear Non-Proliferation Treaty, see Pierre Goldschmidt, "Safeguards Noncompliance: A Challenge for the IAEA and the U.N. Security Council," *Arms Control Today* 40 (January-February 2010), pp. 2–27.

22. Pierre Goldschmidt, "Enforcing the Nuclear Nonproliferation Treaty and International Atomic Energy Agency Compliance," in *Reviewing the Nuclear Nonproliferation Treaty,* edited by Henry Sokolski (Carlisle, Pa.: Strategic Studies Institute, Army War College, 2010), pp. 423–41.

23. Rebecca Bornstein, "Enforcing a Nuclear Disarmament Treaty," in *Elements of a Nuclear Disarmament Treaty,* edited by Blechman and Bollfrass, p. 161.

24. Jonathan Schell, "The Abolition," in *The Fate of the Earth and the Abolition,* edited by Jonathan Schell (Stanford University Press, 2000).

25. Bruce G. Blair, *Global Zero Alert for Nuclear Forces* (Brookings, 1995).

26. Although its comments on the subject are offered only in passing, the Obama administration appears to agree with this concept of maintaining certain reconstitution capabilities even after the elimination of nuclear weapons; see Robert M. Gates, *Nuclear Posture Review Report* (Department of Defense, April 2010), p. 42.

27. See, for example, Frederic S. Nyland, "Exemplary Industrial Targets for Controlled Conflict," in *Strategic Nuclear Targeting,* edited by Desmond Ball and Jeffrey Richelson (Cornell University Press, 1986), p. 215.

28. Christopher A. Ford, "Why Not Nuclear Disarmament?" *New Atlantis* 27 (Spring 2010), p. 5.

29. Perkovich and Acton, *Abolishing Nuclear Weapons,* pp. 104–06.

Chapter Five

1. International Panel on Fissile Materials, *Global Fissile Material Report 2009: A Path to Nuclear Disarmament* (New York: 2009), p. 80 (www.fissilematerials.org [April 5, 2010]).

2. Michael E. O'Hanlon, *Neither Star Wars Nor Sanctuary: Constraining the Military Uses of Space* (Brookings, 2004), pp. 105–17.

3. Robert M. Gates, *Nuclear Posture Review Report* (Department of Defense, April 2010), p. 21. In fact, the treaty allows another 100 non-deployed launchers, and because each nuclear-capable bomber counts as carrying just one warhead regardless of actual loading, the treaty also allows additional warheads to be carried on bombers.

4. Robert S. Norris and Hans M. Kristensen, "Nuclear Notebook: U.S. Nuclear Forces, 2007," *Bulletin of the Atomic Scientists* (January–February 2007), pp. 79–82; Robert S. Norris and Hans M. Kristensen, "Russian Nuclear Forces, 2008," *Bulletin of the Atomic Scientists* (May–June 2008), p. 55.

5. On the idea of major White House involvement, see Stephen J. Blank, *Russia and Arms Control: Are There Opportunities for the Obama Administration?* (Carlisle, Pa.: Strategic Studies Institute, Army War College, 2009), p. 120.

6. Joshua M. Epstein, *Measuring Military Power* (Princeton University Press, 1984), p. 174; Raymond Hall, David Mosher, and Michael O'Hanlon, *The START Treaty and Beyond* (Congressional Budget Office, 1991), pp. 22–24.

7. David Cortright and Raimo Vayrynen, *Towards Nuclear Zero* (London: International Institute for Strategic Studies, 2010), pp. 75–77.

8. See, for example, Hui Zhang, "China's Perspective on a Nuclear-Free World," *Washington Quarterly* 33 (April 2010), p. 143; and T. P. Sreenivasan, "Bringing India's Dream to Fruition," *Washington Quarterly* 33 (April 2010), pp. 169–79.

9. Because safe command and control of nuclear forces is obviously an imperative, this treaty process should at least give some attention to cybersecurity. Within the Department of Defense, the Air Force has been focused on creating the "24th Air Force" under Air Force Space

Command as one part of a clearer bureaucratic focus on these key issues. See Rebecca Grant, "The Cyber Menace," *Air Force Magazine* (March 2009), p. 27.

10. Steven Pifer, "Reversing the Decline: An Agenda for U.S.-Russia Relations in 2009," Foreign Policy Paper Series 10 (Brookings, January 2009) (www.brookings.edu [February 10, 2009]).

11. Bruce G. Blair, "De-Alerting Strategic Forces," paper presented at the "Reykjavik II" conference, Hoover Institution, Stanford, Calif., October 2007, p. 4.

12. On warhead estimates, see Robert S. Norris and Hans M. Kristensen, "Nuclear Notebook: U.S. Nuclear Forces, 2009," *Bulletin of the Atomic Scientists* 65 (March-April 2009), p. 61.

13. Under the New START Treaty, all intercontinental ballistic missiles (ICBMs) will be deployed with just one warhead apiece. See Gates, *Nuclear Posture Review Report*, p. 23. See also Alexei Arbatov and Rose Gottemoeller, "New Presidents, New Agreements? Advancing U.S.-Russian Strategic Arms Control," *Arms Control Today* 38 (July-August 2008), p. 10. The Minuteman ICBM force is expected to be functional until perhaps 2030, possible even 2050, with some upgrading and other upkeep such as replacing the solid propellants of the missiles along the way. See Dana J. Johnson, "Strategic Nuclear Triad Force Structure Study: Maximizing Deterrent Value" (Arlington, Va.: Northrop Grumman Analysis Center, June 30, 2009), p. 4, briefing presented to author on June 30, 2009; and John A. Shaud, *In Service to the Nation: Air Force Research Institute Strategic Concept for 2018–2023* (Maxwell Air Force Base, Ala.: Air University Press, January 2009), p. 35.

14. International Institute for Strategic Studies, *The Military Balance 2008* (London: 2008), p. 29; Energy Secretary Samuel W. Bodman and Defense Secretary Robert M. Gates, "National Security and Nuclear Weapons in the 21st Century" (Department of Energy and Department of Defense, September 2008), p. 16 (www.defenselink.mil/news/nuclear weaponspolicy.pdf [September 25, 2008]).

15. Amy F. Woolf, "U.S. Strategic Nuclear Forces: Background, Developments, and Issues" (Congressional Research Service, August 5, 2008) (http://assets.opencrs.com/rpts/RL33640_20080805.pdf [September 5, 2008]); Michael E. O'Hanlon, *The Science of War* (Princeton University Press, 2009), pp. 5–50.

16. Lora Saalman, "How Chinese Analysts View Arms Control, Disarmament, and Nuclear Deterrence after the Cold War," in *Engaging*

China and Russia on Nuclear Disarmament (Monterey, Calif.: Monterey Institute of International Studies, 2009), p. 71; for a Chinese viewpoint discussing these matters see Major General Pan Zhenqiang (ret.), "China's Nuclear Strategy in a Changing World Strategic Situation," in *Unblocking the Road to Zero: China and India*, edited by Barry M. Blechman (Washington: Henry L. Stimson Center, March 2009), pp. 43–52 (www.stimson.org/nuke/pdf/UnblockingRoadZeroChinaIndia.pdf [July 1, 2009]).

17. On various aspects of the policies of the George W. Bush administration, see Hans M. Kristensen, "White House Guidance Led to New Nuclear Strike Plans against Proliferators" (Washington: Federation of American Scientists, November 2007) (www.fas.org/blog/ssp/2007/11 [December 22, 2009]).

18. Joint Chiefs of Staff, *National Military Strategy* (Department of Defense, 1992), p. 13.

19. See, for example, White House, *A National Security Strategy for a New Century* (October 1998), p. 12.

20. "NATO Reactions on No First Use," *Arms Control Today* (November-December 1998) (www.armscontrol.org/print/423 [December 22, 2009]).

21. Canberra Commission, "Report of the Canberra Commission on the Elimination of Nuclear Weapons," Executive Summary (Canberra: March 1996), p. 5 (www.ccnr.org/canberra.html [December 1, 2009]).

22. Gates, *Nuclear Posture Review Report*, pp. 26–27.

23. For recent discussion of this issue, see East-West Institute, "Reframing Nuclear De-Alert: Decreasing the Operational Readiness of U.S. and Russian Arsenals" (New York: 2009) (www.ewi.info [November 15, 2009]).

24. The Obama administration has not yet broached such changes; see Gates, *Nuclear Posture Review Report*, pp. 27–28, 32.

25. Jayantha Dhanapala, "Rebuilding an Unraveled Consensus for Sustainable Nonproliferation," in *Breaking the Nuclear Impasse*, edited by Jeffrey Laurenti and Carl Robichaud (New York: Century Foundation, 2007), pp. 24–25.

26. See Comprehensive Test Ban Treaty Organization Preparatory Commission website (www.ctbto.org/the-treaty/status-of-signature-and-ratification [April 15, 2010]).

27. India in particular may still have doubts about the effectiveness and reliability of its deterrent force; see T. S. Gopi Rethinaraj, "Bang

or Whimper? Reconsidering India's Nuclear Capabilities," *Jane's Intelligence Review* (December 2009), pp. 48–53.

28. George P. Shultz, William J. Perry, Henry A. Kissinger, and Sam Nunn, "A World Free of Nuclear Weapons," *Wall Street Journal*, January 4, 2007, p. A15.

29. Daryl G. Kimball, "Learning from the 1999 Vote on the Nuclear Test Ban Treaty," *Arms Control Today* 39 (October 2009), pp. 46–52.

30. See, for example, John P. Caves Jr., "Avoiding a Crisis of Confidence in the U.S. Nuclear Deterrent," *Strategic Forum* 252 (January 2010) (www.ndu.edu/inss [March 1, 2010]).

31. Michael A. Levi, "Dreaming of Clean Nukes," *Nature* 428 (April 29, 2004), p. 892.

32. Jean du Preez, "A South African Perspective on the Nuclear Postures of the Five NPT Nuclear Weapons States," paper presented at Stanford University conference "P-5 Nuclear Doctrines and Article VI" (October 16–17, 2007), p. 153; Wisconsin Project on Nuclear Arms, "South Africa's Nuclear Autopsy," January–February 1996 (www.wisconsin project.org/countries/safrica/autopsy.html [April 6, 2010]).

33. Zhang Hui, "Revisiting North Korea's Nuclear Test," *China Security* 3 (Summer 2007), pp. 119–30.

34. Daniel Clery, "Test Ban Monitoring: No Place to Hide," *Science* 325 (July 24, 2009), p. 385.

35. Trevor Findlay and Andreas Persbo, "Watching the World," *Bulletin of the Atomic Scientists* (March–April 2005), pp. 58–63; "Status of Certified IMS Facilities," *CTBTO Spectrum* 11 (September 2008), p. 17; Preparatory Commission for the Comprehensive Nuclear Test Ban Treaty Organization, "The CTBT Verification Regime: Monitoring the Earth for Nuclear Explosions" (Vienna: 2009).

36. David Hafemeister, "The Comprehensive Test Ban Treaty: Effectively Verifiable," *Arms Control Today* 38 (October 2008), p. 8.

37. Preparatory Commission for the Comprehensive Nuclear Test Ban Treaty Organization, "The CTBT Verification Regime: Monitoring the Earth for Nuclear Explosions"; Tibor Toth, "Building Up the Regime for Verifying the CTBT," *Arms Control Today* 39 (September 2009), p. 8.

38. Steve Fetter, *Toward a Comprehensive Test Ban* (Cambridge, Mass.: Ballinger, 1988), pp. 107–58.

39. Roddam Narasimha, "Putting a Stop to Nuclear Madness," paper presented at Stanford University conference "P-5 Nuclear Doctrines and Article VI" (October 16–17, 2007), p. 187; Rajesh M. Basrur,

"Indian Perspectives on the Global Elimination of Nuclear Weapons," in *Unblocking the Road to Zero: China and India,* edited by Blechman, pp. 1–27 (www.stimson.org/nuke/pdf/UnblockingRoadZeroChinaIndia.pdf [August 1, 2009]).

40. Kurt M. Campbell, Robert J. Einhorn, and Mitchell B. Reiss, eds., *The Nuclear Tipping Point* (Brookings, 2004).

41. For a somewhat dated but still useful discussion of Indian strategic debates, see Ashley J. Tellis, "Toward a 'Force-in-Being': The Logic, Structure, and Utility of India's Emerging Nuclear Posture," in *Journal of Strategic Studies: Special Issue on India as an Emerging Power,* edited by Sumit Ganguly 25 (December 2002), pp. 61–108.

42. James Cotton, "North Korea and the Six-Party Process: Is a Multilateral Resolution of the Nuclear Issue Still Possible?" *Asian Security* 3 (2007), pp. 36–37.

43. Richard L. Garwin, "A Different Kind of Complex: The Future of U.S. Nuclear Weapons and the Nuclear Weapons Enterprise," *Arms Control Today* 38 (December 2008) (www.armscontrol.org/act/2008_12/Garwin [September 1, 2009]); William J. Broad, "Panel Sees No Need for A-Bomb Upgrade," *New York Times,* November 20, 2009 (www.nytimes.com/2009/11/20/us/20nuke.html?_r=1&pagewanted=print [December 1, 2009]).

44. "At the Workbench: Interview with Bruce Goodwin of Lawrence Livermore Laboratories," *Bulletin of the Atomic Scientists* (July-August 2007), pp. 46–47; A. Fitzpatrick and I. Oelrich, "The Stockpile Stewardship Program: Fifteen Years On" (Washington: Federation of American Scientists, April 2007), pp. 48–55 (www.fas.org/2007/nuke/Stockpile_Stewardship_Paper.pdf [June 1, 2009]).

45. National Nuclear Security Administration, "Reliable Replacement Warhead Program" (Washington, March 2007) (www.nnsa.doe.gov/docs/factsheets/2007/NA-07-FS-02.pdf [January 1, 2009]).

46. Keir Lieber and Daryl Press, "The Nukes We Need," *Foreign Affairs* 88 (November-December 2009), p. 41.

47. Walter Pincus, "Gates Suggests New Arms Deal with Russia," *Washington Post,* October 29, 2008, p. A8; speech by Secretary of Defense Robert M. Gates at the Carnegie Endowment for International Peace, Washington, October 28, 2008 (www.defenselink.mil/speeches/speech.aspx?speechid=1305 [July 1, 2009]).

48. Walter Pincus, "New Nuclear Warhead's Funding Eliminated," *Washington Post,* May 24, 2007, p. A6.

49. National Nuclear Security Administration, "NNSA Budget, FY 2009" (Washington, 2008) (http://nnsa.energy.gov/management/nnsa_budget.htm [February 10, 2009]).

50. Steve Fetter and Frank von Hippel, "Does the United States Need a New Plutonium-Pit Facility?" *Arms Control Today* 34 (May 2004) (www.armscontrol.org/act/2004_05/fettervonHippel [September 22, 2008]).

51. Zia Mian and A. H. Nayyar, "Playing the Nuclear Game: Pakistan and the Fissile Material Cutoff Treaty," *Arms Control Today* 40 (April 2010), pp. 17–24.

52. Cortright and Vayrynen, *Towards Nuclear Zero*, pp. 131–32.

53. The treaty should cover naval nuclear reactors employing highly enriched uranium as well as the stockpiles of excess fissile materials in military inventories (which exceed those in actual weapons for the United States and Russia). See Arend Meerburg and Frank N. von Hippel, "Complete Cutoff: Designing a Comprehensive Fissile Material Treaty," *Arms Control Today* 39 (March 2009), pp. 16–23.

54. See, for example, Louise Frechette, "The New Nuclear Century," *Global Brief: World Affairs in the 21st Century* (May 2009), p. 67 (www.globalbrief.ca [December 1, 2009]); for more on the additional protocol, see International Atomic Energy Agency, "Fact Sheet: IAEA Safeguards Overview" (Vienna: undated) (www.iaea.org/Publications/Factsheets/English/sg_overview.html [December 1, 2009]); see also Christopher A. Ford, "Five Plus Three: How to Have a Meaningful and Helpful Fissile Material Cutoff Treaty," *Arms Control Today* 39 (March 2009), pp. 27–28.

55. For relevant ideas, see Paul Lettow, *Strengthening the Nuclear Nonproliferation Regime* (New York: Council on Foreign Relations, 2010), pp. 22–24.

56. Frank von Hippel, "Spent-Fuel Management: The Cases of Japan, South Korea, and Russia," in *Multinational Approaches to the Nuclear Fuel Cycle,* edited by Charles McCombie, Thomas Isaacs, Noramly Bin Muslim, Tariq Rauf, Atsuyuki Suzuki, Frank von Hippel, and Ellen Tauscher (Cambridge, Mass.: American Academy of Arts and Sciences, 2010), pp. 32–35.

57. President Barack Obama, speech in Prague, April 5, 2009 (www.whitehouse.gov/the_press_office/Remarks-By-President-Barack-Obama-In-Prague-As-Delivered/ [December 1, 2009]).

58. John Steinbruner, "Engagement with Russia: Managing Risks, Repairing Rifts," *Arms Control Today* 39 (January-February 2009), p. 9.

59. Philip E. Coyle, "Oversight of Ballistic Missile Defense (Part 3): Questions for the Missile Defense Agency," testimony before the House Committee on Oversight and Government Reform, Subcommittee on National Security and Foreign Affairs, 110 Cong. 2 sess. (April 30, 2008), p. 12 (www.cdi.org/pdfs/CoyleTestimonyApr08.pdf [July 29, 2008]).

60. For an example of Russian thinking on missile defenses, see Major General Pavel S. Zolotarev, "Approaches to Reducing the Risk of Nuclear Multi-Polarity," in *Future of the Nuclear Security Environment in 2015: Proceedings of a 2007 Russian-U.S. Workshop,* edited by Ashot A. Sarkisov and Rose Gottemoeller (Washington: National Academies Press, 2009), pp. 233–34.

61. "DoD News Briefing with Lt. Gen. Trey Obering," July 15, 2008, pp. 2–3 (www.defenselink.mil/transcripts/transcript.aspx?transcriptid= 4263 [August 1, 2008]); Ronald O'Rourke, "Sea-Based Ballistic Missile Defense—Background and Issues for Congress" (Congressional Research Service, May 23, 2008), pp. 13, 40 (www.fas.org/sgp/crs/weapons/RL337 45.pdf [August 1, 2008]).

62. Rear Admiral Alan B. Hicks, "Seabased Ballistic Missile Defense," *Joint Forces Quarterly* 50 (2008), pp. 43–45.

63. Philip E. Coyle, "Oversight of Ballistic Missile Defense (Part 2): What Are the Prospects; What Are the Costs?" testimony before the House Committee on Oversight and Government Reform, Subcommittee on National Security and Foreign Affairs, 110 Cong. 2 sess. (April 16, 2008), pp. 17–18.

64. Ann Scott Tyson, "U.S. Shoots Down Missile in Simulation of Long-Range Attack," *Washington Post,* December 6, 2008, p. A2.

65. Warren Ferster, "Airborne Laser Conducts 1st Integrated Test Firing," *Space News,* September 15, 2008, p. 8.

66. Col. Robert McMurry and Lt. Gen. Michael Dunn, "Airborne Laser: Assessing Recent Developments and Plans for the Future" (Washington: George C. Marshall Institute, June 27, 2008), pp. 1–9 (www. marshall.org/pdf/materials/593.pdf [August 2, 2008]).

67. Walter Slocombe, undersecretary of defense for policy, "U.S. Limited National Missile Defense Program," presentation at Harvard-CSIS Ballistic Missile Defense Conference, Cambridge, Mass., May 2000, p. 27; reprinted in *Defending America: The Case for Limited National Missile Defense,* edited by James M. Lindsay and Michael E. O'Hanlon (Brookings, 2001), p. 6.

68. For a similar view, see Ellen Tauscher, "European Missile Defense: A Congressional Perspective," *Arms Control Today* 37 (October 2007), p. 12.

69. George N. Lewis and Theodore A. Postol, "The Technological Basis of Russian Concerns," *Arms Control Today* 37 (October 2007), pp. 13–18.

70. Nick Brown, Daniel Wasserbly, Andrew White, and Martin Streetly, "Long-Rangers: Expanding Reach of Theatre-Wide Air Defence," *Jane's International Defence Review* (January 2010), pp. 48–53.

71. Arbatov and Gottemoeller, "New Presidents, New Agreements? Advancing U.S.-Russian Strategic Arms Control," pp. 12–14.

72. Lewis and Postol, "The Technological Basis of Russian Concerns," pp. 17–18.

INDEX